Michelin wins the 2003 World Rally Championship

Michelin celebrates our 18th World Manufacturers title with Team Citroën Total, as well as passing a world record of 200 WRC victories. We race for tyre perfection. For the track or for you, every Michelin tyre shares this strength. Now you know why Michelin races ahead.

Share the Spirit

RALLY YEARBOOK
World Rally Championship

2003

CHRONOSPORTS
EDITEUR

WORLD RALLY CHAMPIONS 2003.

Petter Solberg in his Pirelli shod Subaru is the new World Rally Champion Driver.
A celebration of Pirelli's 19th World Rally Championship title.

POWER IS NOTHING WITHOUT CONTROL.

RALLY YEARBOOK
World Rally Championship

2003

Photography
DPPI

Words
Philippe Joubin
Jean-Philippe Vennin "Rallyes Magazine"

Artistic Director
and page layout
Cyril Davillerd

Translated from french by
David Waldron

Coordination
Cyril Davillerd, Andre Vinet

Results
Tino Cortese, André Vinet, Cyril Davillerd

ISBN 2-84707-049-4
© November 2003, Chronosports S.A.
Jordils Park, Chemin des Jordils 40, CH-1025 St-Sulpice, Switzerland.
Tel. : (+41 21) 694 24 44. Fax : (+41 21) 694 24 46.
e-mail: info@chronosports.com   internet: www.chronosports.com

Printed and bound by Partenaires in France.

For me it's not only an honour but also an immense pleasure to write the preface to the Rally Yearbook. It really drives home the fact that I'm world champion. And it can only be a good thing as I haven't quite come to terms with the fact that I AM WORLD CHAMPION!

The Sunday of the British Rally was the greatest day of my life, after that of my son's birth! It was just unbelievable. Right up to the finishing line I tried not to think about the championship and what was at stake. But afterwards it was really crazy!

Of course, this season was not all highs: there were difficult moments as well but I was convinced that we could beat the French teams this year. I would like to thank the whole Subaru team as they never gave up and always believed in our chances even when I brought them back a completely destroyed Subaru from the Corsica shakedown: And of course the people from Pirelli.

I would also like to thank Pernilla who became Pernilla Solberg this year for her unwavering support. Also my co-driver Phil Mills by my side for four years now: we won that title together. And finally Tommi Mäkinen who over the past two years had become much more than just a team-mate, a real friend in fact. It is difficult to imagine how precious it was for me to have him in the squad. I wish him the same happiness in his new life as he found in the world of rallying.

Next year I was hoping to team up with Richard Burns with whom I'd driven in 2000 and 2001. Unfortunately his illness will prevent him from joining us. I'd like him to know that we are all thinking of him and we are impatient to see him back among us.

Roll on next year. I'll do my very best to be back here on this page in 2004.

Petter Solberg

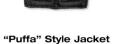

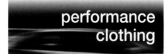

Contents

Stable mate's all out battle

Although Peugeot and Citroën belong to the same group they were given the green light to go head to head in the Rally World Championship. The battle went down to the wire and the newcomer finally overcame its sister firm 3-times winner of the championship. Petter Solberg, however, reaped the benefits of this inter-company struggle by winning the drivers' title.

It would not be true to say the two French teams exercised a complete stranglehold on the 2003 Rally World Championship. Although they were at each other's throats throughout the season for the manufacturers' title winning ten rallies (five each) out of fourteen Petter Solberg won the drivers' title in his Subaru Impreza and Markko Märtin showed he was the quickest driver of the pack once he got his hands on the new Ford Focus.

Citroën: a stunning exploit

At the beginning of the season not many people would have dared to predict that the 'other PSA Company' would become champion on a wintry Sunday afternoon in Wales in its first full season

In fact, Citroën gave itself the resources to achieve its aim. Its much-awaited entry on the world scene was meticulously organised according to a well thought out plan. The firm took part in four rallies in 2001 (first victory in the Tour of Corsica with Jesus Puras) and eight in 2002 (plus additional more or less semi-official entries and reconnaissance for each event by Sébastian Loeb when he was not racing) followed by the full fourteen in 2003.

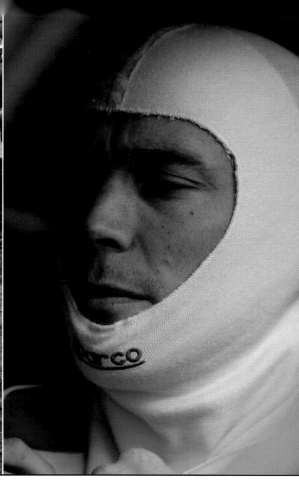

All the Xsara's weaknesses had been ironed out even if its development seemed to flag a little in 2002. Guy Fréquelin, however, pulled not one but two rabbits out of the hat for the 2003 season by hiring two legendary drivers that Ford either didn't want or couldn't keep. Colin McRae signed for the French manufacturer at the end of 2002 and Carlos Sainz did the same only a few weeks before Monte Carlo helped by the backing of a big Spanish sponsor.

Fréquelin, a fervent defender of limiting entries to two cars per team, had to revise his plans and created a dream team that had little to envy Peugeot. Thanks to the input from the newcomers the Xsara progressed by leaps and bounds on gravel and won its first event on this surface in Turkey. The car's reliability, Sébastian Loeb's talent, Carlos Sainz's steadiness and the errors of its rivals did the rest.

Media wise the team orders given to Sébastian Loeb in Great Britain to ensure victory in the Manufacturers' Championship put a damper on Citroën's triumph. These prevented the Alsatian from fighting for the drivers' crown up to the bitter end. However, even if winning one of the titles (above all the manufacturers' one) this year was not the objective that the team set itself Citroën could not have let the chance slip. On arriving in Wales the French team knew which one was the easiest to win. Sébastian's day will come.

Peugeot: failure

For Peugeot 2003 was a failure. The Sochaux company has always won at least one title since its debut in WRC: two in 2000 and 2002 and one in 2001. In 2003 it ended the season empty-handed even though the 206 painted in a new livery, that of a famous cigarette company whose sponsorship it had spirited away from Citroën, did not seem to be outpaced in terms of sheer performance. In the hands of Marcus Grönholm it was the car that was best able to match the pace of the Ford Focus.

On the other hand, it suffered from the same unreliability as on its debut, which prevented its drivers from getting the best out of it. Harri Rovanperä screwed up his season while Gilles Panizzi saved his in San Remo and above all in Catalonia though neither seemed on the same wavelength as the management.

Marcus Grönholm, winner of three rallies, made too many unenforced errors as in Australia and San Remo. Richard Burns brought the most points to the team thanks to his steadiness, as he had

understood that for him anyway it would be impossible to win in the 206. This raises the question: was the 206 WRC outclassed this year despite the declarations to the contrary of Corrado Provera, the Peugeot Sport boss? Maybe Burns was right after all while Grönholm compensated by overdriving. Sometimes it works, sometimes it doesn't or as the French say: "ça passe ou ça casse!"

Perhaps, the Peugeot team underestimated its rivals. Or overestimated the capacity of the 206 to remain competitive for another season without further development as priority was given to the 307.

Subaru, Ford: the right gamble

For the second time in three years a Subaru driver won the drivers' title. Despite Tommi Mäkinen's presence in the team all the efforts were invested in Petter Solberg. He had already pushed Burns very hard in 2001, and quickly got the measure of the 4-times world champion the following year. Even so it would be a bit of an exaggeration to say that Solberg accelerated Mäkinen's retirement as he had been thinking about it since his departure from Mitsubishi two years earlier. On the other hand the advice that Tommi gave to the young Norwegian was such that he deserves credit for part of the latter's success as does the rest of the Subaru team members.

Solberg had that necessary little bit of luck mainly in the Tour of Corsica. His mechanics managed to rebuild a squashed Impreza just in time for the start and then it rained at the end creating just the right conditions for his Pirellis. The rest of the time the Subaru was as solid as a rock apart from a suspension problem in Turkey and gremlins in the fuel feed in Italy. Petter has a reputation for crashing but this year he went off only once when he hit ice in Monte Carlo. That also was one of the keys of his success.

Ford too won its bet if not a title. The make scored two victories thanks to rising start Markko Märtin. Malcolm Wilson faced with a reduced budget from Ford plus the departure of his two major sponsors gambled on developing a completely new Focus (designed by Belgian Christian Loriaux) and on youth with Markko Märtin (27) and François Duval (22), Mikko Hiroven (22) and Jari-Matti Latvala (a young 18-year-old Finn!) for a limited programme.

The car was very quick but reliability problems prevented Märtin from battling for the title. Above all its success has done nothing to resolve the team's financial problems and it has again been hit by a budgetary reduction so a question mark hangs over its presence in 2004.

2 0 0 4 : S o
w h a t ' s n e w ?

2003 was symptomatic of the problems created by the rise in costs in the WRC and the gap between the big and small teams widened. Ford's example shows that even winning is no guarantee for the future.

The FIA seemed obsessed with increasing the number of events to 16 whatever the price adding Japan and Mexico to the calendar. It also rattled on about reducing costs. Thus the teams can enter only two cars to score points in the Manufacturers' Championship and the reconnaissance and sweeper vehicles will be banned.

Skoda will take part in 10 events and the absence of Hyundaï will be compensated for by the return of Mitsubishi (which took a year off in 2003 to recharge its batteries). Let us hope that despite a smaller field the battle for the championships will be as exciting as ever.

CITROËN WORLD RALLY CHAMPION 2003

CITROËN

www.citroen.com

Petter Solberg

Words: Anthony Peacock, rallyXS.

Despite fluffing his lines on the first three rallies of 2003, Petter solberg believes that it is not yet too late for him to take centre stage in the race for the world championship

Petter Solberg bursts into the room like an effervescent blond cyclone of hyperactive energy. His stream-of-consciousness narrative never misses a beat as he effortlessly flits from person to person, propelled by a wave of handshakes and musical Norwegian laughter. Everyone wants their own piece of shrink-wrapped Nordic megastar.

World rallying without Petter would be like Breakfast at Tiffany's without Audrey Hepburn. It's not surprising he is nicknamed 'Hollywood'. The looks complement the reputation: he has the finely-chiselled features of a silver screen icon of the 1950s, allied with the blond mop of an '80s New Romantic. The world, and a fawning bevy of beautiful women, is at his feet.

You could even write a decent film script of his life to date: from humble beginnings as Norwegian disco dancing champion, he becomes an overnight sensation with Ford's world rally team. Subaru poaches him in a mid-season coup one year later, but our hero marks the occasion by crashing on five of his first seven rallies. The closing credits loom. But with the help of a psychologist he rebuilds his confidence.

Podiums follow, but it's a slow and painstaking process. Then he wins the Rally Great Britain in a shower of champagne, mud, sweat and tears. The End.

Except Solberg hopes this is just the beginning. His win was a momentous occasion: Subaru's service area resembled

Iron Maiden's mosh pit; his omnipresent fan club risked a group coronary; and there were more tears shed than at the premiere of Watership Down.

Petter rode the roller coaster of celebrity last year and climbed off at the end second overall in the World Rally Championship. There is only one place to go from there, but it's getting harder and harder to be the world champion in a sport that is suddenly full of bright young things like Markko Martin, Sebastien Loeb and Francois Duval.

The early rallies of 2003 were not the start to a championship-winning campaign that he had hoped for. But let's get this straight, he always believed he could win the title this year. "There's no reason why it shouldn't be possible," he said after trhee events. " Everyone knows Peugeot is strong, but we are trying to beat them and this might be the right year. Subaru know how to make world champions. I've got a good feeling about everything right now."

This 'good feeling' is something that the Norwegian talks a lot about. He admits he has an emotional personality that thrives on human contact. He loves to be loved. At Subaru, he has a strong relationship with team principal David Lapworth, who has extracted the best from his young charge.

"We could see in Petter what we saw in the young Colin McRae," says Lapworth. "It was just a question of him finding the balance between speed and risk. When Petter first joined us, he was going out there and trying to beat everybody. What we did was change his whole strategy. He

and I talked it through, and we decided that he should just drive for safety and forget about the result.

Gradually, we were able to build up his confidence and introduce a greater element of risk. With all the really quick drivers - such as Marcus [Gronholm] and Colin [McRae] - their natural speed carries an element of risk. You'll never get away from that."

There are some big differences between Petter and the other drivers, though. He's not as thick-skinned as the hardened veterans. He sees his role in the team as going beyond just driving the car. He doesn't retreat into the motorhome every time he encounters a paying member of the species homo sapiens; you'll often see him having tea with his mechanics in service; and he'll always buy you a drink at the post-rally party. He is not the sort to sit in his hotel with room service. He's constantly visible.

"You can't just be a driver and nothing else," he says. "You need to think of the whole team. Everybody is together for such a long time that it's like a family. We all have different personalities, but I really want to share myself with all the people who are working with me: the mechanics, the journalists, the PR people, the caterers - everyone. Nobody should be left out. Life is so short and you never know what is happening tomorrow. Enjoy everyone while you can, you know?"

It's an impromptu but heartfelt little sermon that underlines the value that he attaches to human relationships. A lot of

that is down to his gregarious upbringing. As a youngster, he spent much of the yea living in an old bus with his parents as they toured the Norwegian rallycross circuit. Their rallycross cars were hardly state-of-the-art (Petter reckons that they cost about £500 each), but the young Solberg had finally discovered what he wanted to do. He applied himself with customary ambition ("I was always the first into the workshop each morning and the last to leave each night"), but never dreamed he would come as far as he has. Not that it has really changed him. He spends his time at home in Norway surrounded by family, including baby son Oliver. (Petter describes Oliver as "completely crazy" - we can't possibly imagine where he gets that from.) Solberg family life revolves around motorsport. They race around frozen fields in winter with old VW Beetles, Saabs - whatever they can get their hands on. "Motorsport i 24 hours in all the family," says Solberg. "My mother, my father, my brother, my girlfriend, her parents, her uncles, my uncles..."

While on the world championship, where it's all somewhat more serious, Petter relies on his Subaru family. The three mos important professional relationships that will get him through the next critical months are those with team boss Lapworth, co-driver Phil Mills and team-mate Tommi Makinen.

Mills is the person who knows Petter the best, having occupied the seat beside him since 1999. They've shared some great

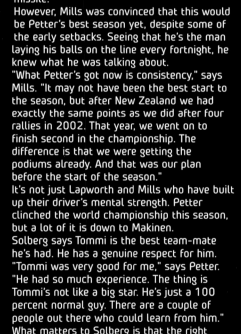

times – Phil remembers crying for much of the road section home after winning the Rally GB in his native Wales. They've also shared some scary times – the Welshman equally remembers becoming a freelance lumberjack when Solberg launched their Ford Focus at some Finnish trees in 2000. At full speed, with the casual precision of an unguided missile.

However, Mills was convinced that this would be Petter's best season yet, despite some of the early setbacks. Seeing that he's the man laying his balls on the line every fortnight, he knew what he was talking about.

"What Petter's got now is consistency," says Mills. "It may not have been the best start to the season, but after New Zealand we had exactly the same points as we did after four rallies in 2002. That year, we went on to finish second in the championship. The difference is that we were getting the podiums already. And that was our plan before the start of the season."

It's not just Lapworth and Mills who have built up their driver's mental strength. Petter clinched the world championship this season, but a lot of it is down to Makinen.

Solberg says Tommi is the best team-mate he's had. He has a genuine respect for him. "Tommi was very good for me," says Petter. "He had so much experience. The thing is Tommi's not like a big star. He's just a 100 percent normal guy. There are a couple of people out there who could learn from him." What matters to Solberg is that the right people believe in him. It means he doesn't have to worry. He just lets it flow, drives naturally. And it works !

PETTER SOLBERG - PHILIP MILLS
SUBARU IMPREZA WRC 2003
RALLY OF CYPRUS

7

THE STARS

PETTER SOLBERG
SUBARU

IDENTITY CARD
- Nationality: Norwegian
- Date of birth:
  November 18, 1974
- Place of birth:
  Spydeberg (Norway)
- Marital status: Married, 1 child
- Co-driver: Phil Mills (British)

- Web: www.pettersolberg.com

CAREER
- First Rally: 1996
- Number of Rallies: 60
- Number of victories: 5

1999 - 18th in championship
2000 - 10th in championship
2001 - 9th in championship
2002 - 2nd in championship
2003 - WORLD CHAMPION

This was the year when the new generation of drivers took over in the WRC led by Petter Solberg who won the drivers' title. Had it been Sébastian Loeb it would not have been a miscarriage of justice but finally the Norwegian was the first to upset the established apple cart.

As soon as Solberg arrived on the rally scene in 1999 in Malcolm Wilson's Ford squad his raw speed was obvious. Initially he made a lot of mistakes but these soon became increasingly rare and it was Subaru that took full advantage of his talent. Success was long in coming and he did not win his first rally until Great Britain in 2002, which gave him a flattering last-minute second place in the championship behind the untouchable Marcus Grönholm. His 2003 season got off to a bad start with two retirements in three rallies (accident in Monte Carlo and suspension problems in Turkey) but he then finished all the rest. Petter's three victories were not down to his biggest asset, his top speed as he came home first on the stones of Cyprus then in Corsica where the wet asphalt on the final leg was just the job for his Pirellis; and finally on the tricky Welsh roads. Before the French round, though he almost lost everything in a huge accident in which his car was badly damaged but thanks to his courage and willpower, a little bit of luck, and the efforts of his whole team, he came out on top.

SÉBASTIEN LOEB
CITROËN

RICHARD BURNS
PEUGEOT

At the start of the year the signs were obvious that Petter Solberg would be world champion one day. And the same could be said of Sébastian Loeb. 2003 was the Alsatian's first full year in the world championship (fourth for the Norwegian) in a works car. Loeb almost repeated the same exploit as Marcus Grönholm in 2000. The Finn, though, had been rallying for much longer as it should be remembered that Loeb sat in a rally car for the first time in 1996.

He did not necessarily lose the title in Great Britain when Citroën ordered him to ensure the make's victory in the Manufacturers' Championship as he had let slip a few opportunities earlier in the season. Maybe it was in Catalonia when he made the wrong tyre choice due to a lack of communication between his team and Michelin which cost him victory in a rally that he dominated as well as two precious points as in the he lost the title by just one! He also crashed in Corsica losing ten minutes when his car got stuck in a ditch. He won in Monte Carlo, Germany and Italy on roads that were made for him but it was in Australia that he really showed his mettle gaining everybody's respect and admiration by matching the pace of the future world champion. He did exactly the same thing in Wales destroying drivers like Tommi Mäkinen and Colin McRae without even going flat out.

It would be an understatement to say that Richard Burns' collaboration with Peugeot was a setback. He did not win any rallies in the WRC 206 that he so much wanted to drive after winning the title for Subaru in 2001. Initially he was attracted to the Peugeot because of its dimensions, agility and performance but he was unable to adapt to the driving position and had problems integrating himself into the team. In addition, he was completely dominated by Marcus Gronholm.

However, Burns led the championship for most of the year, which was not always an advantage as he was the first to sweep the track for the others on the opening day of the rally. Knowing that he would have great difficulty in winning he opted for regularity and scored several rostrum placings. This tactic was favoured by the new points system and he was often criticised for it but after all was it not the same for Carlos Sainz who won in Turkey using the same approach. Burns set more scratch times in specials than the Spaniard and again shone on the very quick Finnish roads.

Richard Burns was supposed to rejoin Subaru for 2004. After collapsing just before the British rally and being forbidden to take part he was effectively eliminated from the title chase. Doubts have been cast on his capacity to race in 2004 but hopefully he will be back in 2005.

IDENTITY CARD
- Nationality: French
- Date of birth: February 26, 1974
- Place of birth: Haguenau (France)
- Resident: Oberhoffen (France)
- Marital status: Single
- Co-driver: Daniel Eléna (Monaco)

- Web: www.fanloeb.com

CAREER
- First Rally: 1995
- Number of Rallies: 36
- Number of victories: 4

2002 - 10th in championship
2003 - 2nd in championship

IDENTITY CARD
- Nationality: British
- Date of birth: January 17, 1971
- Place of birth: Reading (England)
- Resident: Oxford (England)
- Marital status: Single
- Co-driver: Robert Reid (British)

- Web: www.richardburns.com

CAREER
- First Rally: 1990
- Number of Rallies: 103
- Number of victories: 10

1994 - 19th in championship
1995 - 9th in championship
1996 - 9th in championship
1997 - 7th in championship
1998 - 6th in championship
1999 - 2nd in championship
2000 - 2nd in championship
2001 - WORLD CHAMPION
2002 - 5th in championship
2003 - 4th in championship

MARCUS GRÖNHOLM
PEUGEOT

MARKKO MÄRTIN
FORD

Markko Märtin was made no.1 driver of the Ford team after the departures of Colin McRae and Carlos Sainz who had been the strike force of the blue oval since 1998 and 1999 respectively. He did more than fulfil his role. He was the third member of the 'nouvelle vague' with Loeb and Solberg and did a fantastic job in developing the new Focus WRC03. He scored his first two wins in Greece and Finland and others escaped him due to the car's unreliability, which prevented him from being a title contender. He only lost his head once (in Corsica) where he went off on several occasions. He has what it takes to be world champion. Why not in 2004?

IDENTITY CARD
- Nationality: Estonian
- Date of birth: November 11, 1975
- Place of birth: Tartu (Estonia)
- Resident: Tartu
- Marital status: Single
- Co-driver: Michael Park (British)

CAREER
- First Rally: 1994
- Number of Rallies: 51
- Number of victories: 2

1998 - Not classified
1999 - 18th in championship
2000 - 21th in championship
2001 - 17th in championship
2002 - 9th in championship
2003 - 5th in championship

CARLOS SAINZ
CITROËN

"His only chance of finding a drive is with Citroën," as we wrote a year ago in the Rally Yearbook when Carlos Sainz, recently dropped by Ford, looked like he was on his way to premature retirement. He got the drive and made more out of it than Colin McRae who had chosen the same squad.
Carlos won in Turkey in a new rally as he had done in Cyprus in 2000, lost in Argentina due to a misunderstanding with his new co-driver and was still in the frame for the title at the start of the final round. He has been one of the sport's great ambassadors as well as its most professional driver and he will do another season before hanging up his hat at the end of 2004.

Years ending in uneven numbers do not agree with Marcus Grönholm. He dominated in 2000 and 2002 winning the drivers' title both times and lost out in 2003 as in 2001 due to a mixture of personal errors (lack of concentration?), mechanical failures and bad luck. He is still one of the quickest drivers if not THE quickest and his pace has not suffered in comparison with the young guns, as has that of McRae and Mäkinen. The Finn sometimes overdoes it and makes unenforced mistakes like those in Great Britain in 2002 and Australia 2003 which have cost him wins and prevented him from getting close to the record number of victories (25 for Sainz and McRae) one that he looked like breaking not so long ago.

IDENTITY CARD
- Nationality: Finnish
- Date of birth: February 5, 1968
- Place of birth: Espoo (Finland)
- Resident: Inkoo (Finland)
- Marital status: Married, 3 children (Jessica, Johanna and Niclas)
- Co-driver: Timo Rautiainen (Finnish)

- Web: www.mgr.fi

CAREER
- First Rally: 1989
- Number of Rallies: 85
- Number of victories: 14

1996 - 10th in championship
1997 - 12th in championship
1998 - 16th in championship
1999 - 15th in championship
2000 - WORLD CHAMPION
2001 - 4th in championship
2002 - WORLD CHAMPION
2003 - 6th in championship

IDENTITY CARD
- Nationality: Spanish
- Date of birth: April 12, 1962
- Place of birth: Madrid (Spain)
- Resident: Madrid (Spain)
- Marital status: Married, 3 children (Bianca, Carlos and Ana)
- Co-driver: Marc Marti (Spain)

- Web: www.carlos-sainz.com

CAREER
- First Rally: 1987
- Number of Rallies: 179
- Number of victories: 25

1988 - 11th in championship
1989 - 8th in championship
1990 - WORLD CHAMPION
1991 - 2nd in championship
1992 - WORLD CHAMPION
1993 - 8th in championship
1994 - 2nd in championship
1995 - 2nd in championship
1997 - 3rd in championship
1998 - 2nd in championship
1999 - 4th in championship
2000 - 3rd in championship
2001 - 5th in championship
2002 - 3rd in championship
2002 - 3rd in championship

COLIN McRAE
CITROËN

2003 was a bit of a disappointment as was last year at Ford. This year McRae, who not long ago was the best-known rally driver thanks to the video game bearing his name, was part of the Citroën squad. He was never the quickest of the Xsara trio and was systematically beaten by Loeb or Sainz or both. Finally, McRae, who was the youngest-ever Rally World Champion, finished his season without a win for the first time since 1993.

McRae never lacked motivation and was a hard worker bringing precious points to the French team in its conquest of the world title. Alas, it was not enough for him to retain his seat with the new regulations restricting the teams to two cars in 2004.

IDENTITY CARD
- Nationality: British
- Date of birth: August 5, 1968
- Place of birth: Lanark (Scotland)
- Resident: Scotland, Monaco
- Marital status: Married, 1 daughter
- Co-driver: Derek Ringer (British)

- Web: www.colinmcrae.com

CAREER
- First Rally: 1986
- Number of Rallies: 143
- Number of victories: 25

1992 - 8th in championship
1993 - 5th in championship
1994 - 4th in championship
1995 - WORLD CHAMPION
1996 - 2nd in championship
1997 - 2nd in championship
1998 - 3rd in championship
1999 - 6th in championship
2000 - 4th in championship
2001 - 2nd in championship
2002 - 4th in championship
2003 - 7th in championship

GILLES PANIZZI
PEUGEOT

Gilles ended his sojourn at Peugeot which goes back to the very beginning of his career (with a few exceptions) by scoring a memorable win in Catalonia where he choose exactly the right tyres and caught and passed Sébastian Loeb. He had already almost done the same thing at San Remo but elsewhere his driving lacked conviction. In Monte Carlo and Germany he seemed absent and not at all in the right frame of mind. Perhaps he was disappointed by what he felt was a lack of confidence in him by his team which refused him a drive in the whole championship. However, the 'king of the asphalt' drove some of his best rallies on gravel! He came fifth in Turkey and finished ahead of the works cars of Rovanperä and Loix in Wales in a private 206 entered by the Bozian team. In 2004 Mitsubishi will profit from his experience.

IDENTITY CARD
- Nationality: French
- Date of birth: September 19, 1965
- Place of birth: Roquebrune Cap Martin (France)
- Resident: Monaco
- Marital status: Married, 1 dauthter
- Co-driver: Hervé Panizzi (French)

- Web: www.club-panizzi.com

CAREER
- First Rally: 1990
- Number of Rallies: 53
- Number of victories: 7

1997 - 9th in championship
1998 - 12th in championship
1999 - 10th in championship
2000 - 7th in championship
2001 - 7th in championship
2002 - 6th in championship
2003 - 10th in championship

TOMMI MÄKINEN
SUBARU

IDENTITY CARD
- Nationality: Finnish
- Date of birth: June 26, 1964
- Place of birth: Puupola (Finland)
- Resident: Puupola and Monaco
- Marital status: Single, 1 son (Henry)
- Co-driver: Kaj Lindström (Finnish)

- Web: www.tommimakinen.net

CAREER
- First Rally: 1984
- Number of Rallies: 139
- Number of victories: 24

Those who say that Tommi Makinen did one or maybe two years too many got it wrong. While his two years at Subaru did not bring him the same success as his four with Mitsubishi his experience was a godsend to the team and his young team-mate Petter Solberg for whom he became a mentor. His love of driving was obvious and his rostrum finish in Great Britain in his last rally was a just reward. He has left an indelible mark on rallying being the only driver to have won four consecutive Driver World Championship titles between 1996 and 1999 an achievement that merits the same acclaim as Michael Schumacher's successes. Life is not always fair but that does not bother Tommi!

1990 - 20th in championship
1991 - 29th in championship
1993 - 10th in championship
1994 - 10th in championship
1995 - 5th in championship
1996 - WORLD CHAMPION
1997 - WORLD CHAMPION
1998 - WORLD CHAMPION
1999 - WORLD CHAMPION
2000 - 5th in championship
2001 - 3rd in championship
2002 - 8th in championship
2003 - 9th in championship

FREDDY LOIX
HYUNDAI / PEUGEOT

The Belgian, who will be with Peugeot in 2004, must feel that he come back from hell. In his second season with Hyundai after a good performance in 2002 he must have thought that he was reliving the nightmare years between 1999 and 2001 with Mitsubishi. The reasons, however, were not the same. The Anglo-Korean team was bled white by political and financial conflicts, could not develop its Accent WRC and threw in the sponge with four rallies still to go, Loix's best place up to then being eighth. Freddy was called up to replace Burns in the 206 for the Rally GB and did a good job as he beat Rovanperä (who retired) in the same car, which may have precipitated the Finn's fall from grace.

IDENTITY CARD
- Nationality: Belgian
- Date of birth: November 10, 1970
- Place of birth: Tongres (Belgium)
- Resident: Millen (Belgium)
- Marital status: Singel
- Co-driver: Sven Smeets (Belgian)
- Web: www.freddyloix.com

CAREER
- First Rally: 1993
- Number of Rallies: 89
- Best result: 2^e

1996 - 8th in championship
1997 - 9th in championship
1998 - 8th in championship
1999 - 8th in championship
2000 - 12th in championship
2001 - 11th in championship
2002 - 17th in championship
2003 - 14th in championship

FRANÇOIS DUVAL
FORD

The young Belgian driver (Solberg, Loeb and Märtin seem like old hands in comparison) did not appear to fulfil the hopes placed in him by the man who gave him his break at this level, Malcolm Wilson. François, though, was on the rostrum twice, once in Turkey in a new rally where previous experience did not count and he could have won in Corsica thus achieving the objective set for him by his boss if it had not rained on the last day. The latter did not hesitate in putting pressure on him and openly criticised him for certain mistakes (in Finland for example) due to a rather haphazard note taking system even though his co-driver was the experienced Stéphane Prévot, Bruno Thiry's former sidekick.

IDENTITY CARD
- Nationality: Belgian
- Date of birth: November 18, 1980
- Place of birth: Chimary (Belgium)
- Marital status: Single
- Co-driver: Jean-Marc Fortin (Belgian) then Stéphane Prévot (Belgian)
- Web: www.fduval.com

CAREER
- First Rally: 1999
- Number of Rallies: 35
- Best result: 3^e

2002 - 30th in championship
2003 - 8th in championship

HARRI ROVANPERÄ
PEUGEOT

In 2002 Harri finished second four times scoring precious points for Peugeot when Grönholm or Burns fell by the wayside or were let down by their cars. This year he flattered only to deceive. He found himself in the same ambiguous position as Gilles Panizzi in the Peugeot team and was restricted to gravel events. His best rally was in Cyprus where he finished second in a damaged 206 that he had repaired himself. In Great Britain he failed to play his expected part in the battle for the manufacturers' title and was dropped by the French team after being confirmed for 2004 before the event!

IDENTITY CARD
- Nationality: Finnish
- Date of birth: April 8, 1966
- Place of birth: Jÿvaskÿla (Finland)
- Resident: Jÿvaskÿla
- Marital status: Married, 1 child
- Co-driver: Risto Pietiläinen (Finnish)
- Web: www.rovanpera.com

CAREER
- First Rally: 1989
- Number of Rallies: 77
- Number of victories: 1

1999 - 9th in championship
2000 - 9th in championship
2001 - 4th in championship
2002 - 7th in championship
2003 - 11th in championship

Frenchman Brice Tirabassi won the title in this championship reserved for driver under twenty-eight years of age after Sébastian Loeb in 2001 and Dani Solà from Spain in 2002. They both drove Citroëns to victory while Tirabassi was at the wheel of a Renault Clio. He won in Monte Carlo, Greece and Spain but had to wait until the final round to clinch the title as he was still under threat from Spaniard Salvador Canellas. The latter never won a round but was the steadiest. His Suzuki team-mate Swede Daniel Carlsson (hired by Peugeot for 2004) finished third with two victories.
Mirco Baldacci (Fiat Punto) and Kosti Katajamaki (VW Polo) each won a round.

Tirabassi - Renucci, Canellas & Carlsson.

Bugalski, Hirvonen, Robert & Kresta.

DIDIER AURIOL
SKODA

Didier Auriol was back after a year off following his divorce from Peugeot at the end of 2001 while his fellow-countryman François Delacour was left on the sidelines by the provisional withdrawal of Mitsubishi. The 1994 World Champion was not afraid to set himself another challenge even if he had already had a bad experience with SEAT in 2000. He retired six times this year (once before the first special (!) plus one withdrawal because of injury). None, though, was due to error on his part. The little Fabia was the big disappointment: it arrived too late and was very underpowered scoring worse results than the tried and tested Octavia. Like his team-mate his best result, sixth, was in a rally he likes, Argentina.

IDENTITY CARD
- Nationality: French
- Date of birth: August 18, 1958
- Place of birth: Montpellier (France)
- Resident: Millau (France)
- Marital status: Married, 2 children (Robin and Diane)
- Co-driver: Denis Giraudet (French)

CAREER
- First Rally: 1984
- Number of Rallies 150
- Number of victories: 20

1988 - 6th in championship	1996 - 25th in championship
1989 - 4th in championship	1997 - 11th in championship
1990 - 2nd in championship	1998 - 5th in championship
1991 - 3rd in championship	1999 - 3rd in championship
1992 - 3rd in championship	2000 - 12th in championship
1993 - 3rd in championship	2001 - 6th in championship
1994 - WORLD CHAMPION	2002 - Not participated
1995 - Excluded (Toyota)	2003 - 13th in championship

ARMIN SCHWARZ
HYUNDAI

This is probably the German driver's final season as he had few illusions about finding a better drive than Hyundaï in 2004 until the Korean company decided to pull the plug on its rallying programme before the San Remo round. His only results of note were eighth in the Monte Carlo event and seventh in Cyprus due more to the raft of retirements than the intrinsic competitiveness of his Accent. For a long time he was notorious for his accidents but this year his only terminal shunt was in New Zealand and he was generally let down by his car's lack of reliability. Difficult to remain motivated in such conditions. Germany still awaits a champion to embody the growing success of WRC rallying at home.

IDENTITY CARD
- Nationality: German
- Date of birth: July 16, 1963
- Place of birth: Oberreichenbach (Germany)
- Resident: Monaco
- Marital status: Married
- Co-driver: Manfred Hiemer (D)
- www.armin-schwarz.com

CAREER
- First Rally: 1988
- Number of Rallies: 100
- Number of victories: 1

1991 - 6th in championship
1994 - 7th in championship
1995 - Excluded (Toyota)
1997 - 8th in championship
1999 - Not classified
2000 - 17th in championship
2001 - 11th in championship
2002 - 24th in championship
2003 - 18th in championship

Philippe Bugalski spent most of his year testing for Citroën and was entered for the four events on asphalt, his task being to try and take points off Loeb and Sainz's direct rivals. He scored just one in San Remo.
Young Finn Mikko Hiroven the third Ford driver did the full season but in a 2002 car. He did not make many mistakes but did not make much of an impression either except in Corsica where he set one scratch time in the rain. Best result: 6th in Cyprus.
Cédric Robert drove a WRC 206 entered by the Bozian team in Monte Carlo (6th) and Germany (9th) but the French hope was offered nothing concrete by Peugeot for 2004.
Last but not least the young Czech Roman Kresta who also drove a private 206. He set two scratch times in Germany and Spain and should be driving a Skoda next year.

Rowe

Arai, Blomqvist, Singh, Solà

TONI GARDEMEISTER
SKODA

Toni Gardemeister still has to fulfil his promise and he has not been helped by never having a car in which to show his talent. His only challenge was to beat his more experienced team-mate Didier Auriol and his performances did not suffer in comparison to those of the Frenchman. The new Skoda Fabia WRC failed to live up to his expectations. His seven retirements included three accidents (San Remo was not his fault). His few eye-catching performances were at the wheel of the old, heavy but reliable Skoda Ovtavia which gave him four top 10 finishes including a fifth in New Zealand where he had finished third in 2000 in a SEAT. Toni has accumulated a lot of experience but the reductions in the number of drives in 2004 has prevented him from finding a seat in a better car in the near future.

IDENTITY CARD
- Nationality: Finnish
- Date of birth: March 31, 1975
- Place of birth: Kouvola (Finland)
- Resident: Monaco and Kouvola
- Marital status: Single
- Co-driver: Paavo Lükander (SF)

CAREER
- First Rally: 1997
- Number of Rallies: 61
- Best result : 3e

1999 - 10th in championship
2000 - 12th in championship
2001 - Not classified
2002 - 13th in championship
2003 - 12th in championship

Martin Rowe, the former British champion in a Renault Mégane has not had the same success as his friend Richard Burns. However, he won the Production Car World Championship title this year in a Mitsubishi after a tough duel with Toshihiro Araï from Japan in a Subaru. Rowe was victorious only once but scored six rostrum finishes out of seven (those not counting for the Junior Championship). Araï was victorious three times but racked up the same number of retirements. The unsinkable Stig Blomqvist (1984 world champion in an Audi Quattro) won on home turf in Sweden in his Mitsubishi and Catalonian Dani Solà (the reigning Junior champion) came first in Italy.

BIG BROTHER

THE CAR IN THE PICTURE IS ON STAGE 18 OF THE RALLY TURKEY – MILES FROM THE SERVICE PARK AND DEEP IN THE ANATOLIAN MOUNTAINS. WITH THE AID OF INMARSAT'S SATELLITE TECHNOLOGY, THE TEAM CAN MONITOR THE CAR'S PROGRESS IN REAL-TIME

Inmarsat thrives on challenges and in motorsport terms they don't come much bigger than providing coverage of the FIA World Rally Championship (WRC). The global partnership between Inmarsat and the WRC, then, is not a only natural one, but also key to the success of the sport.

Rallies are held in the most remote parts of the world and the WRC pits the greatest rally drivers against environments that test both man and machine to their limits. It is important to implement an information network that can communicate with the world: stage times have to be recorded, teams need to know their standing in the rally, and photographers and journalists have to file their photographs and stories.

Inmarsat and its satellite communications provide a lifeline for teams, organisers and fans at each rally, because many local telecom companies or GSM mobile phone networks often do not work. Inmarsat's supply of GAN (Global Area Network) terminals to both Rally HQ and the event's Service Park is not only global, but has reliability and network availability in excess of 99.99%.

Timing of rally cars used to be reliant on a finger on a stop watch. Now satellites orbiting the earth carry out this function. As the cars reach the end of each stage, individual times will be automatically relayed over thousands of miles. To make the service even more valuable to the WRC fraternity, Inmarsat has also developed a system by which data can be beamed from each car, at any position on the stages, to the rally base and, ultimately, the driver's crew. This information not only allows the teams to monitor the performance of each car, but if there's an accident or a breakdown and the car stops unexpectedly, then it makes it easier to maintain the highest standards of safety.

It is not only the teams competing in the WRC who are benefiting from Inmarsat's ground-breaking technology. The rally fans watching the television images at home have access like never before. With the advent of Channel 4's 'Virtual Spectator', the daily rally round-up programme uses a set of unique graphics that track the progress of each car over the stages, relative to its competitors.

The WRC might visit some of the most inhospitable places in the world, but thanks to Inmarsat's revolutionary communications network news of what is happening, when it's happening, is now available immediately.

Inmarsat, exclusive global partner to the FIA WRC providing vital timing and data communication around the world

MARCUS GRÖNHOLM – TIMO RAUTIAINEN
PEUGEOT 206 WRC
RALLY OF SPAIN

WRC
FIA WORLD RALLY
CHAMPIONSHIP

1

MARCUS GRÖNHOLM – TIMO RAUTIAINEN
PEUGEOT 206 WRC
RALLY OF SPAIN

WRC
FIA WORLD RALLY
CHAMPIONSHIP

TARMAC OR GRAVEL

MONTE CARLO OR WALES

AP RACING LEADS THE WAY WITH SUPER 1600 EQUIPMENT

The experience gained in product development with leading WRC teams has been carefully adapted to suit the requirements of Super 1600 rallying.

A specially designed Super 1600 caliper to suit discs from Ø355mm down to Ø295mm is complemented by a range of discs, pedal boxes, cylinders and robust, lightweight clutches all at an affordable price.

A call now to our technical sales department will give you all the information you need.

AP RACING

WHELER ROAD

COVENTRY

CV3 4LB

ENGLAND

TEL **+44 (0)24 7663 9595**

FAX +44 (0)24 7663 9559

EMAIL: sales@apracing.co.uk

AP RACING

THE SCIENCE OF FRICTION

www.apracing.com

THE TEAMS

CITROËN XSARA WRC

Engine
- Type: DOHC
- Disposition: front transverse
- Number of cylinders: 4
- Capacity: 1,998 cc
- Camshaft: double overhead
- Bore x stroke: 86 x 86 mm
- Power: 300 bhp at 5500 rpm
- Maximum torque: 520 Kgs/m
- Valves: 4 per cylinder
- Turbo: Garrett
- Lubrification: carbon wet sump
- Gestion: Magnetti-Marelli

Transmission
- Clutch: carbone tri-disc 140 mm
- Gearbox: longitudinal 6-speed
  X-Trac sequential
- Differentials: programmable

Suspensions
- Front and rear: McPherson-type
- Dampers: Extremetech

Brakes
- Front: ventilated discs (304 mm diametre),
  4-piston calipers
  For asphalt use: discs (368 mm,
  6-piston calipers)
- Rear: ventilated discs (304 mm diametre),
  4-piston calipers

Tyres
- Michelin

Dimensions
- Wheelbase: 2555 mm
- Lenght: 4167 mm
- Widht: 1770 mm
- Rims: OZ 8 x 18'''
- Weight: 1230 kg

Web
- www.citroensport.com

For a first attempt Guy Fréquelin's team pulled off a masterstroke by winning the manufacturers' world title (its first in proper rallying after several in the less prestigious rally raids) in its first full season like Peugeot three years before. The French team's success was due in part to its cars' exemplary reliability as in forty-two starts (3 cars in 14 rallies) there were only 3 retirements because of mechanical problems: engine for Loeb in Greece, suspension for McRae in New Zealand and fire for him in Argentina while Sainz was never let down by his car. The Citroën had undergone a thorough test programme and was maybe a little slower than the Ford. In the mid-term the Xsara should be replaced by the future C4 (2005?).

Positions
- 1982 - 12th
- 1983 - 14th
- 1984 - 13th
- 1985 - 18th
- 1986 - 10th
- 2001 - not classified
- 2002 - not classified
- 2003 - 1st

PEUGEOT 206 WRC

Positions
- 1973 - 3rd
- 1973 - 15th
- 1974 - 13th
- 1975 - 5th
- 1976 - 8th
- 1977 - 13th
- 1978 - 8th
- 1979 - 11th
- 1980 - 8th
- 1981 - 9th
- 1983 - 10th
- 1984 - 3rd
- 1985 - 1st
- 1986 - 1st
- 1988 - 10th
- 1993* - 3rd
- 1994* - 5th
- 1995* - 1st
- 1996* - 4th
- 1997* - 3rd
- 1998* - 2nd
- 1999 - 6th
- 2000 - 1st
- 2001 - 1st
- 2002 - 1st
- 2003 - 2nd

(* = 2 litres)

Web
- www.peugeot.com

Engine
- Type: XU9J4
- Disposition: front transverse
- Number of cylinders: 4 in line
- Capacity: 1997,5 cm^3
- Camshaft: double overhead
- Bore x stroke: 85 x 88 mm
- Power: 300 bhp at 5250 rpm
- Maximum torque: 535 kgs/m at 3500 rpm
- Cylinder head: aluminium
- Valves: 4 per cylinder
- Cylinder block: aluminium
- Engine management: Magneti Marelli
- Turbo: Garrett Honeywell
- Lubrification: carbon wet sump

Transmission
- Clutch: 5.5" ou 6" AP carbon tri-disc
- Gearbox: longitudinal 6-speed X-Trac sequential
- Differentials: programmable

Suspensions
- Front and rear: McPherson
- Dampers: Peugeot

Steering
- Power-assisted rack and pinion

Brakes
- Front: ventilated discs (370 mm diametre), 8-piston calipers
- Rear: ventilated discs (370 mm diametre), 4-piston calipers

Tyres
- Michelin 20x65x18"

Dimensions
- Wheelbase: 2468 mm
- Lenght: 4005 mm
- Widht: 1770 mm
- Height: 1370 mm
- Rims: OZ 8 x 18"
- Weight: 1230 kg
- Fuel tank capacity: 85 litres

Corrado Provera the Peugeot Sport boss hammered home the fact that in 2003 the 206 was not as down on power as its results indicated. The times set, particularly by Marcus Grönholm, tended to prove him right. However, the triple world champion team which had never been beaten over a full season since its debut suffered from poor reliability and a certain lack of bite on the part of its two third drivers Rovanperä and Panizzi allied to Grönholm's errors. The Peugeot squad was a little optimistic by no longer updating the 206 and concentrating all its efforts on the new 307 that will defend its colours in 2004. But then how much more was there to come especially when faced with new generation cars like Ford?

FORD FOCUS RS WRC 02 /03

This is probably the benchmark car at the moment. The Ford Focus WRC03 from the pen of the Belgian engineer Christain Loriaux (ex-Subaru) stands out because of its looks, which are reminiscent of a circuit racer. This proved a drawback as its very low front spoiler had an annoying tendency to pick up stones and dead leaves causing overheating. Other mechanical gremlins stopped it too often but once Markko Märtin got his hands on it in the New Zealand rally he became the quickest driver whatever the surface. Ford's bet, namely, to get rid of its stars McRae and Sainz and concentrate its limited budget on the car and young drivers paid off. Alas, this has not solved the team's financial problems.

SUBARU IMPREZA WRC 2003

Engine
- Type: flat 4-cylinder, 16 valve
- Number of cylinders: 4
- Capacity: 1,994 cc
- Bore x stroke: 92 x 75 mm
- Power: 300 bhp at 5500 rpm
- Torque: 60 kgs/m at 4000 rpm
- Turbo Charger: IHI

Transmission
- Gearbox: Prodrive 6-speed electro-hydraulic semi-automatic
- Differentials: electro-hydraulically controlled

Suspensions
- Front: McPherson strut
- Rear: McPherson strut with longitudinal and transverse link

Dampers
- Bilstein

Steering
- Power assisted rack and pinion

Brakes
- Front and rear: ventilated discs (305 mm diametre), 4-pot calipers
- for asphalt use: 366 mm ventilated discs with 6-pot water cooled calipers.

Tyres Pirelli

Dimensions
- Wheelbase: 2535 mm
- Lenght: 4415 mm
- Width: 1770 mm
- Rims: OZ 8 x 18"
- Weight: 1230 kg
- Fuel tank capacity: 80 litres

Web www.swrt.com

The same tactics that Subaru had used two years earlier with Richard Burns paid off for Petter Solberg. The Japanese team entered only two cars throughout the season and thinking that Mäkinen was a bit past it did not go for the manufacturers' title concentrating instead on the drivers' crown for the Norwegian who had assumed the mantle of team leader in 2002. By a stroke of good/bad? fortune it was Mäkinen who was hit with most of the mechanical problems as Solberg retired only twice for the same reasons. With a well-developed car and the presence of Richard Burns Subaru looked like a very serious contender for the 2004 manufacturers' title and a danger to the French squads but the Englishman's absence because of illness will weaken its challenge.

Positions
1983 - 7th	1990 - 4th	1997 - 1st
1984 - 9th	1991 - 6th	1998 - 3rd
1985 - 12th	1992 - 4th	1999 - 2nd
1986 - 8th	1993 - 3rd	2000 - 3rd
1987 - 10th	1994 - 2nd	2001 - 3rd
1988 - 9th	1995 - 1st	2002 - 3rd
1989 - 12th	1996 - 1st	2003 - 3rd

Positions
1973 - 3rd	1980 - 3rd	1988 - 2nd	1996 - 3rd
1974 - 3rd	1980 - 8th	1989 - 13th	1997 - 2nd
1975 - 6th	1981 - 3rd	1990 - 8th	1998 - 4th
1976 - 3rd	1982 - 4th	1991 - 4th	1999 - 4th
1977 - 2nd	1984 - 12th	1992 - 3rd	2000 - 2nd
1978 - 2nd	1985 - 11th	1993 - 2nd	2001 - 2nd
1979 - 1st	1986 - 5th	1994 - 3rd	2002 - 2nd
	1987 - 5th	1995 - 3rd	2003 - 4th

Engine
- Type: Ford Duratec R
- Number of cylinders: 4
- Capacity: 1,998 cc
- Bore x stroke: 85 x 88 mm
- Power: 300 bhp at 6500 rpm
- Maximum torque: 550 Nm at 4000 rpm
- Engine management: Pi electronic
- Turbo: Garrett
- Lubrification: carbon wet sump

Transmission
- Clutch: Sachs
- Gearbox: XTrac 240 6-speed sequential gearbox with electro-hydraulically controlled shift
- Differentials: M-Sport

Suspensions
- Front and rear: McPherson
- Dampers: Reigher

Steering
- Power-assisted high ratio (12:1) rack and pinion

Brakes
- Front and rear: 300mm Brembo ventilated discs, 4-piston calipers

Tyres
- Michelin

Dimensions
- Wheelbase: 2615 mm
- Lenght: 4442 mm
- Widht: 1770 mm
- Height: 1420 mm
- Weight: 1230 kg

Web www.fordracing.net

SKODA
OCTAVIA WRC EVO 3
FABIA WRC

More was expected of the Skoda team which has become the more or less official arm of the VAF Group in WRC. Extra money has been allocated and the team's ambitions upgraded as witnessed by the arrival of a new car aping the 206 and aimed at erasing the memory of the heavy, bulky Octavia. The Fabia appeared in Germany but obviously lacked horsepower and suffered from erratic reliability so the only team it managed to beat was Hyundai. Perhaps early claims were over-optimistic. The new engine never arrived and in 2004 Skoda will only race in the European events effectively ruling itself out of contention for the championship titles as a team has to do all the rounds to score points.

Positions
- 1993* - 2nd
- 1994* - 1st
- 1995* - 3rd
- 1996* - 3rd
- 1997* - 2nd
- 1999 - 7th
- 2000 - 6th
- 2001 - 5th
- 2002 - 5th
- 2003 - 5th

Engine
- Type: 4 cylinders
- Capacity: 1,999 cc
- Bore x stroke: 82,5 x 93,5 mm
- Power: 220 bhp at 5500 rpm
- Maximum torque: 600 kg/m at 3500 rpm
- Valves: 20
- Turbo: Garrett

Transmission
- Clutch: carbon triple-plate
- Gearbox: 6-speed sequential semi-automatic

Web
www.skoda-auto.com/sport

Suspensions
- Front and rear: McPherson
- Dampers: Proflex

Steering
- Power assisted rack and pinion

Brakes
- Front and rear: disc brakes, internally cooled

Tyres Michelin

Dimensions
- Wheelbase: 2462 mm
- Lenght: 4002 mm
- Widht: 1770 mm
- Weight: 1230 kg

HYUNDAI
ACCENT WRC 3

Will Hyundaï be back in the world championship? Officially yes but not before 2006 with a completely new car and a team based in Germany. The marriage between the Korean manufacturer and the English company MSD is over due mainly to money squabbles. It is a pity as Hyundaï had built up a good reputation since its arrival at the end of the 90s even if its director's ambitions seemed a bit far-fetched. The Accent WRC showed a little promise early on and in 2002 the occasional flash of speed. In 2003, it was completely outclassed despite the energy (of despair?) displayed by its drivers in particular Freddy Loix. Hyundaï was rarely in a position to take advantage of the new points system encompassing the first eight.

Positions
- 1996* - 7th
- 1997* - 6th
- 1998* - 5th
- 1999* - 2nd
- 2000 - 6th
- 2001 - 6th
- 2002 - 4th
- 2003 - 6th

Engine
- Type: DOHC
- Number of cylinders: 4
- Capacity: 1,998 cc
- Bore x stroke: 84 x 90 mm
- Power: 300 bhp at 5200 rpm
- Maximum torque: 520 Kg/m
- Valves: 4 per cylinder
- Turbo: Garrett
- Lubrication: carbon wet sump

Transmission
- Clutch: carbon triple-plate 140 mm
- Gearbox: 6-speed X-Trac sequential semi-automatic
- Differentials: programmable

Suspensions
- Front and rear: McPherson
- Dampers: Ohlins

Brakes
- Front: 304 mm ventilated discs, 4-piston calipers
- For asphalt use: 368 mm, 6-piston calipers
- Rear: 304 mm ventilated discs, 4-piston calipers

Tyres
- Michelin

Dimensions
- Wheelbase: 2440 mm
- Lenght: 4200 mm
- Widht: 1770 mm
- Rims: OZ 8 x 18'''
- Weight: 1230 kg

Web
- www.hyundaiwrc.com

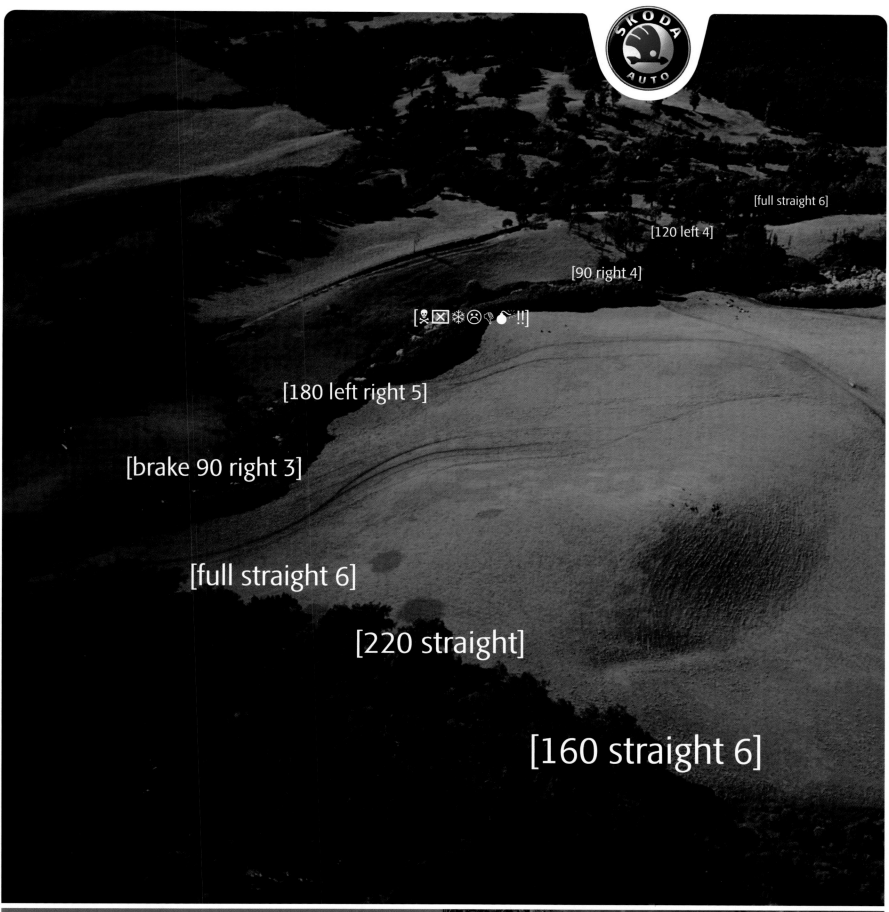

MARKKO MÄRTIN - MICHAEL PARK

FORD FOCUS RS WRC 02

UDDEHOLM SWEDISH RALLY

4

WRC
FIA WORLD RALLY
CHAMPIONSHIP

Monte Carlo

Sébastian Loeb drove a perfect race pressuring the reigning world champion into making a mistake in the second leg. He then took the lead and never looked back. It was his second success in the world championship and it helped Citroën to a triple as he was followed home by team mates McRae and Sainz. Yet again Peugeot screwed up in the opening round.

Marcus Grönholm hates this rally. A good start put him into the lead but an error in Col de Bleine dashed his hopes.

First race for McRae in a Citroën crowned by a second place in a rally where the Scot usually doesn't shine.

THE RACE

One, two, three Xsaras!

Victory was sweet for Loeb after what had happened a year earlier. Monaco, January 2002. The victorious Loeb-Elena Xsara sat atop the rostrum before being pushed back to second a few hours later after being hit by a heavy penalty for a minor fault. While he was the moral winner his name would not go down in the record books.

So Monaco in January 2003 must have given Loeb even greater satisfaction as this time there were no protests from Sabaru to undermine his success as the Citroën drove proudly onto the winner's rostrum. The blue Japanese cars both failed to see the finish.

In 2002, he had beaten one world champion, Tommi Makinen, and this year he fought off another in the person of Marcus Grönholm to score a well-deserved victory.

While the Peugeot driver is no lover of the Monte he was the quickest out of the box bringing a smile to the face of his engineer François-Xavier Demaison: "Marcus flies as soon as his car has studded tyres." There was enough ice and snow on the opening timed specials to justify the fitting of studded rubber on which the Nordic driver's natural skills best express

themselves. He was in his element and drove with the same flair as he shows on the Swedish Rally's ice-bound routes. He immediately opened up a large gap over his pursuers and as Loeb commented:» If he continues at this rhythm I don't know how we're going to catch him."

His performance was a godsend for the reigning world championship team as its other drivers failed to deliver the goods. Gilles Panizzi dropped way down the time sheets and was probably destabilised by the penalty imposed on him before the rally had even begun! His GPS went on the blink

due to a faulty connection during reconnaissance and he was hit with a one-minute handicap before coming under starter's orders. In fact, the brothers had only themselves to blame. Richard Burns had noticed a similar defect and had told the officials thus proving his good faith.

It was Märtin's second Monte and he just missed out on a rostrum finish.

Even the great Tommi, always giving advices to Solberg, had a mishap in his own rally. He missed out on a 5th consecutive victory.

Loeb had a score to settle. Well done.

dog! So one of the favourites was out. Burns too was totally at sea and the Englishman's mediocre performance earned him a good ticking off from his employer. He complained about the poor quality of the food in the Peugeot camp and Corrado Provera hit back with the comment: "a bit like your times!" Luckily, Marcus Grönholm was there to save the Sochaux firm's bacon. He held off his rivals on the first day despite losing time in the two Plan de Vitrolles-Faye specials, the longest in the rally made particularly tricky by snow and ice scattered along the asphalt. Loeb was in maximum risk mode like the Subaru drivers.

In the fifth special Solberg up till then at his very best and Makinen, who had already been slowed by brake problems, both went off in a big way ending their rally. The former Monte Carlo meister made a beginner's mistake, and the young Norwegian took on the parapet of a bridge that proved to be more solid than his Impreza! "Luckily, Peter widened it otherwise our rally would have ended there too," joked a lucky Loeb more than happy to have set the quickest time in this tricky section. It was the same story a few hours later in the same special but this time he dead-heated with Colin McRae. However, on the opening day the young Frenchman completely eclipsed his new, prestigious team-mates, Colin McRae and Carlos Sainz. It was something of an exploit even if the above-mentioned were driving the Citroën for the first time. And as singer Al Jolson once said "You ain't seen nothing yet!"

The second leg looked to favour the hunter rather than the hunted! Loeb was on familiar territory – even though in the first leg he had covered only thirteen kilometres of those programmed – and the Alsatian

He was absolved but not Panizzi. Gilles' mind must have been a bit addled as his choice of tyres was completely wrong for the opening stages: he opted for unstudded rubber a disastrous decision not just in terms of performance but also because of the consequences. He went off in a big

way puncturing two tyres, damaging his 206 WRC and losing a lot of time After that his rally went from bad to worse. His driving was completely awry and he was passed by Martin on the longest stage of the event after which he collapsed physically due to a sudden drop in blood pressure. The

strain of driving, the tension generated by a rally that he wanted to win above all else; the penalty and his technical errors expressed themselves through his body to which was added a debilitating virus. He tried to continue on the second day but retired almost immediately as he was as sick as a

New car, new co-driver, new team. Carlos Sainz's Citroën debut was a success.

Richard Burns did not leave much of a mark on this rally as he was dominated by Marcus Grönholm.

showed the full range of his talent closing the gap between himself and the leader. Marcus had his back up against the wall and tried to put off the inevitable as long as possible. But it all went wrong for the tall Swede in the "Quatre Chemins," the second special of the day he crashed on dry tyres caught out by a patch of ice and twisted a steering arm. He lost thirty minutes repairing it on the spot which put paid to his chances not only of winning but also of a good result. He thought of retiring but his employers ordered him to continue with the slight hope of scoring a single

championship point. Which he did in his usual press-on style. After these incidents the rally was as good as over. McRae and Sainz were both behind Loeb and seeing that any attempt to catch the young Frenchman would be in vain they did not really push preferring to make sure of a Citroën triple.
The Spaniard had his work cut out on the third day as Markko Märtin, weakened by a heavy cold, had driven a fairly anonymous rally since the start. However, the new Ford no.1 was now fighting fit and began to make inroads into the gap separating him

Cédric Robert in a client 206 without the latest mods drove a good rally rewarded by sixth place.

Hyundaï did no winter testing so the Monte was a nightmare for Schwarz (seen here) and Loix.

from Sainz. In addition, Carlos was slowed by a defective wheel bearing, the result of a slight off on the first day. Martin passed the Citroën but Carlos fought back and retook third spot just before the flag giving his employer a remarkable one, two, three. The Ford-mounted Estonian, though, made a big impression certainly helped by his Michelins, as the French manufacturer was now the official Ford tyre supplier. So too did Cédric Robert and Roman Kresta. Although the young Frenchman was further down the classification than Burns he was much more incisive in his client competition 206 while the Czech, also 206 mounted, proved that a well-driven 2001 Peugeot was still a remarkably competitive car. In addition to the Loeb-Citroën combination Tirabassi in his Renault was a happy man at the end of the Monte. The 2002 French champion won the Junior Championship in his Clio Super 1600. Not for a long time had the Monte Carlo rally been such a happy hunting ground for French makes making 2003 a vintage year. ■

A TRIUMPH
The triple

The 2003 Monte Carlo Rally was a turning point for Guy Fréquelin's team as it was the opening event of Citroën's first full world championship season. It was also the team's first race with two new drivers, Colin McRae and Carlos Sainz sharing their cars with co-drivers with whom they had not been used to working in the past, Derek Ringer for the Scot and Marc Marti for the Spaniard. Thanks to five scratch times, a triple and victory for Loeb Citroën could not have dreamed of a better start to the year. In addition, the French make left the Principality with its drivers in the first three places in the Drivers World Champion and eighteen points in the bag in the Manufacturer's one. Before

the start Guy Fréquelin had stated that his objectives in 2003 were: "to win at least three rallies and to finish one of the two championships in at least second place." Obviously, there was still a long way to go but thanks to its performance in the Monte the French team was already well placed to fulfil these objectives. It was a telling victory as the Xsara WRC showed itself to be completely at home on tarmac both in terms both of performance and reliability (the only problem was the defective wheel bearing on Sainz's car following a minor off). The technical backup was also very impressive and no major mistakes were made in the tricky choice of tyres in treacherous conditions. Bravo!

Peugeot left Monaco by the back door as once again the team that had won the 2002 Championships messed up. Panizzi was in the depths of despair, Burns was desperate and only Grönholm emerged with his reputation still intact. Not since 1985 has the Sochaux team won this event when Ari Vatanen triumphed in the mythic 205 Turbo 16. Perhaps it would have been easier for Peugeot to swallow a win by Tommi Makinen in a Japanese car than that of its stable mate, Citroën, as although the two makes are part of the PSA company they are bitter rivals. And to rub salt into Peugeot's wound, Ford with a smaller budget and two inexperienced drivers came away from the first round with more points (ten as against six) in the Manufacturers World Championship. And so as in the past Peugeot was obliged to begin its defence of its titles in the second round in Sweden. "That's a Peugeot tactic, "laughed one of the Citroën team members. "They know that if they want to win in Sweden, they have to lose in Monaco!" Guy Frequelin quipped back. "What's done is done. No problem if they win in Sweden as the media fallout from victory here and one there isn't exactly the same." ■

1st Leg of the 2003 World Rally championship for constructors and drivers 1st Leg of the Junior WRC. championship

Date 23rd to 26th january 2003

Route
1392,03 km divided in 3 legs
14 special stages on tarmac roads (415 km) but 1 contested (382,89 km).

1st leg
Friday 24 January (07h00-22h44):
Gap > Monaco, 708,88 km;
6 special stages (196,30 km)

2nd étape
Saturday 25 January (06h40-16h50):
Monaco > Monaco, 413,99 km;
4 special stages (114,50 km)
but 3 contested (82,39 km)

3rd étape
Sunday 26 January (08h00-15h00):
Monaco > Monaco , 269,16 km;
4 special stages (104,20 km)

Entry List - Starters - Finishers:
56 - 51 - 30

Conditions: dry road, with snowy and icy portions. Then, road mostly dry.

Results

	Driver/Navigator	Car	Gr.	Time
1	**Loeb - Elena**	**Citroën Xsara WRC**	**A**	**4h29'11"4**
2	McRae - Ringer	Citroën Xsara WRC		+ 38"1
3	Sainz - Marti	Citroën Xsara WRC		+ 52"2
4	Märtin - Parck	Ford Focus RS WRC 02		+ 55"5
5	Burns - Reid	Peugeot 206 WRC		+ 3'16"5
6	Robert - Bedon	Peugeot 206 WRC		+ 5'16"7
7	Duval - Fortin	Ford Focus RS WRC 02		+ 5'17"1
8	Schwarz - Hiemer	Hyundai Accent WRC		+ 6'42"3
9	Auriol - Giraudet	Skoda Octavia WRC Evo 3		+ 7'13"8
10	Kresta - Hulka	Peugeot 206 WRC		+ 7'50"9
17	**Tirabassi - Renucci**	**Renault Clio**	**Jr.**	**+ 43'24"7**

Leading Retirements (20)

	Driver/Navigator	Car		
SS9	Loix - Smeets	Hyundai Accent WRC		Accident
SS9	Hirvonen - Lehtinen	Ford Focus RS WRC 02		Accident
SS8	Panizzi - Panizzi	Peugeot 206 WRC		Driver ill
SS5	Mäkinen - Lindstrom	Subaru Impreza WRC 2003		Accident
SS5	Solberg - Mills	Subaru Impreza WRC 2003		Accident
SS2	Gardemeister - Lükander	Skoda Octavia WRC Evo 3		Engine

Brice Tirabassi

Special Stages Times

www.acm.mc
www.wrc.com

SS1 Prunières (28,36 km)
1.Grönholm 18'07"6; 2.Solberg +4"2;
3.C. McRae +8"3; 4.Sainz +9"6;
5.Loeb +14"0; 6.Burns +16"8;
7.Mäkinen +28"1; 8.Märtin +34"1...
Jr. (23) Tirabassi +3'08"6

SS2 Selonnet (22,52 km)
1.Grönholm 16'00"3; 2.C. McRae
+29"4; 3.Mäkinen +31"4; 4.Solberg
+36"7; 5.Loeb +41"2; 6.Burns +44"9;
7.Robert +45"1; 8. Märtin +46"3...
Jr. (18) Carlsson +2'11"9

SS3 Prunières (28,36 km)
1.Loeb 17'54"5; 2.Solberg +6"6;
3.C. McRae +6"9; 4.Grönholm +14"0;
5.Burns +19"5; 6.Märtin +19"6;
7.Duval +21"0; 8.Robert +29"9...
Jr. (22) Baldacci +2'31"6

SS4 Selonnet (22,52 km)
1.Grönholm 15'33"7; 2.Solberg +12"9;
3.Burns +14"2; 4.Loeb +14"4;
5.Sainz +20"3; 6.Kreszta +32"6;
7.Schwarz +33"2; 8.Märtin +33"9...
Jr (19) Carlsson +2'09"5

SS5 Plan de Vitrolles (47,27 km)
1.Loeb 28'54"9; 2.Sainz +17"7;
3.Grönholm +18"3; 4.Märtin +27"3;
5.Burns +32"1; 6.C. McRae +42"9;
7.Robert +1'13"9; 8.Auriol +1'17"3...
Jr. (18) Carlsson +4'26"6

SS6 Plan de Vitrolles (47,27 km)
1.C. McRae/Loeb 30'04"7;
3.Sainz +16"4; 4.Grönholm +16"7;
5.Burns +35; 6.Märtin +38"5;
7.Schwarz +1'10"3; 8.Kresta +1'16"8...
Jr. (17) Carlsson +4'46'9

SS7 Les 4 Chemins (32,11 km)
Cancelled – Too many spectators

SS8 Saint Antonin (25,14 km)
1.Loeb 18'08"0; 2.C. McRae +5"6;
3.Grönholm +7"8; 4.Märtin +7"9;
5.Sainz +9"3; 6.Robert +14"0;
7.Burns +15"3; 8.Duval +21"8...
Jr. (16) Ligato +1'44"5

SS9 Les 4 Chemins (32,11 km)
1.Loeb 24'59"3; 2.Sainz +9"7;
3.Märtin +13"6; 4.C. McRae +14"3;
5.Kresta +22"7; 6.Robert +36"0;
7.Auriol +43"2; 8.Schwarz +1'10"7...
Jr. (14) Baldacci +4'35"2

SS10 Saint Antonin (25,14 km)
1.Sainz 17'52"3; 2.C. McRae +1"1;
3.Märtin +1"9; 4.Grönholm +8"2;
5.Loeb +9"1; 6.Duval +9"6;
7.Robert +10"1; 8.Auriol +12"9...
Jr. (15) Baldacci +2'25"0

SS11 Sospel (32,58 km)
1.C. McRae 25'30"6; 2.Loeb +3"0;
3.Grönholm +14"0; 4.Robert +14"5;
5.Duval +15"9; 6.Märtin +18"8;
7.Sainz +29"5; 8.Kresta +39"1...
Jr. (19) Tirabassi +3'27"1

SS12 Lantosque (19,52 km)
1.Märtin 14'09"4; 2.Duval +2"0;
3.Burns +6"5; 4.Schwarz +18"3;
5.Auriol +26"0; 6.Sainz +37"0;
7.Loeb +49"8; 8.C. McRae +50"1...
Jr. (14) Katajamaki +1'39"3

SS13 Sospel (32,58 km)
1.Sainz 24'52"0; 2.Märtin +4"9;
3.Duval +10"1; 4.C. McRae +22"8;
5.Burns +25"5; 6.Schwarz +28"1;
7.Auriol/Robert +28"9...
Jr. (16) Tirabassi +3'09"1

SS14 Lantosque (19,52 km)
1.Sainz 13'46"1; 2.Märtin +6"7;
3.Duval +12"4; 4.C. McRae +16"6;
5.Robert +19"7; 6.Burns +23"6;
7.Loeb +25"3; 8.Auriol +27"1...
Jr. (14) Baldacci +1'56"3

Performers

	1	2	3	4	5	6
Loeb	5	1	-	1	3	-
Sainz	3	2	1	1	2	1
Grönholm	3	-	3	3	-	-
C. McRae	2	3	2	3	-	1
Märtin	1	2	2	2	-	3
Solberg	-	3	-	1	-	-
Duval	-	1	2	-	1	1
Burns	-	-	2	-	4	3
Mäkinen	-	-	1	-	-	-
Robert	-	-	-	1	1	2
Schwarz	-	-	-	1	-	1
Kresta	-	-	-	-	1	1
Auriol	-	-	-	-	-	2

Event Leaders

SS1 > SS8	Grönholm
SS9 > SS14	Loeb

Previous winners

1973	Andruet - "Biche" Alpine Renault A 110	1985	Vatanen - Harryman Peugeot 205 T16	1995	Sainz - Moya Subaru Impreza 555
1975	Munari - Mannucci Lancia Stratos	1986	Toivonen - Cresto Lancia Delta S4	1996	Bernardini - Andrié Ford Escort Cosworth
1976	Munari - Maiga Lancia Stratos	1987	Biasion - Siviero Lancia Delta HF 4WD	1997	Liatti - Pons Subaru Impreza WRC
1977	Munari - Maiga Lancia Stratos	1988	Saby - Fauchille Lancia Delta HF 4WD	1998	Sainz - Moya Toyota Corolla WRC
1978	Nicolas - Laverne Porsche 911 SC	1989	Biasion - Siviero Lancia Delta Integrale	1999	Mäkinen - Mannisenmäki Mitsubishi Lancer Evo 6
1979	Darniche - Mahé Lancia Stratos	1990	Auriol - Occelli Lancia Delta Integrale	2000	Mäkinen - Mannisenmäki Mitsubishi Lancer Evo 6
1980	Rohrl - Geistdorfer Fiat 131 Abarth	1991	Sainz - Moya Toyota Celica GT-Four	2001	Mäkinen - Mannisenmäki Mitsubishi Lancer Evo 6
1981	Ragnotti - Andrié Renault 5 Turbo	1992	Auriol - Occelli Lancia Delta HF Integrale	2002	Mäkinen - Lindström Subaru Impreza WRC 2001
1982	Rohrl - Geistdorfer Opel Ascona 400	1993	Auriol - Occelli Toyota Celica Turbo 4WD		
1983	Rohrl - Geistdorfer Lancia rally 037	1994	Delecour - Grataloup Ford Escort RS Cosworth		
1984	Rohrl - Geistdorfer Audi Quattro				

Championship Classifications

FIA Drivers (1/14)
1.Loeb 10; 2.C. McRae 8; 3.Sainz 6;
4.Märtin 5; 5.Burns 4; 6.Robert 3;
7.Duval 2; 8.Schwarz 1

FIA Constructors (1/14)
1.Citroën 18; 2.Ford 10; 3.Peugeot 6;
4.Hyundai 3; 5.Skoda 2

FIA Junior WRC (1/7)
1.Tirabassi 10; 2.Katajamäki 8; 3.Ligato 6;
4.Broccoli 5; 5.Aava 4; 6.Ceccato 3;
7.Sebalj 2; 8.Baldacci 1

Sverige

The reigning world champion Marcus Grönholm was unbeatable in Sweden thanks to his skills in tricky conditions and the reliability of his 206 WRC. He dominated a rally in which Tommi Makinen came second after doing his best to hang onto the Finn while third place on the rostrum fell to Richard Burns.

2

Marcus Grönholm completely outshone all his rivals winning this event for the third time.

Citroën's heated tents (here Loeb comes into his bay) were a big boon for the mechanics.

THE RALLY
Grönholm out of reach

A look at the last four years would seem to confirm the adage that a setback in the Monte Carlo in January is rewarded by a win in Sweden; and what if such a success was also a step towards a world championship title at the end of the year as happened in 2000, 2001 and 2002?

Marcus Grönholm's performance in the event was such that it killed the suspense almost as soon as the rally began. Sebastian Loeb again showed his talent and from the start the young Frenchman outshone all his rivals in

the first special on an icy surface that had not yet been covered by a fine layer of snow. As leader of the world championship he had the privilege of starting first which was no handicap. However, after his win in the 14,17 km Sagen special he knew that the

rest of the rally would be a different ballgame as the weather began to worsen. Snow fell just after the end of this stage covering the ground with a fine layer of flakes that played havoc with grip. This time starting first was a big handicap as Loeb, Sainz and

Turkey

Wily old fox Carlos Sainz used all his racecraft and lucidity to score an excellent win in this event, the first for the Xsara WRC on gravel and the twenty-fifth for the Spaniard equalling Colin McRae's record. This was the first time that the event was part of the world championship and the organisers did a great job.

Turkey was new on the calendar and was generally appreciated by all the regulars, Märtin included.

Grönhlom soon ran into power steering problems and did not have a good rally. He scored just one point for his team.

THE RALLY
Sainz unbeatable

The proverb 'the puppy for the path and the old dog for the hard road' sums up the Turkish event as in keeping with a certain tradition in the Rally World Championship it is very often an older and more experienced driver who wins an event on the calendar for the first time. Of course Loeb did win the German Rally in 2002 but like most geniuses he takes a certain pleasure in upsetting the established order of things. Sainz, however, left his rivals no chance in

Turkey having done the same thing in Indonesia seven years earlier and also in Cyprus in 2000. Auriol too won the Chinese rally in 2000 when he was on the wrong side of forty-one. Sainz's main qualities are his race intelligence plus his ability to adapt and during the Indonesian round he paced himself in relation to the two young chargers, Tommi Mäkinen and Colin McRae, until they retired. In Cyprus he found exactly the right compromise between speed and tyre conservation. In Turkey his lucidity and experience plus a helping hand from Dame Fortune brought him victory. The challenge was a tough one, though, as it was his baptism on gravel in the Xsara WRC and only his

Harri Rovanperä held the lead before hitting a rock during the second leg (being pushed by Guy Fréquelin!) and letting Loeb through.

Scwharz took full advantage of his place in the starting order in the first leg and was in second place for a long time.

third event for Citroën as was the case for Marc Marti his co-driver.

In fact, Sainz immediately avoided being caught out by the hazards of this new and very tricky event that was especially hard on the cars. Citroën chief chassis engineer Jean-Claude Vaucard said it was: "between Cyprus and the Acropolis rather than between the Acropolis and Cyprus!" In the third special the power steering on Grönholm's 206 WRC went on the blink and the Finn had to use all his strength to keep the car pointing in the right direction as its steering was about as light as that of an old Saviem lorry! He had to contend with this handicap throughout the first

stage despite having the power steering pump and rack and pinion changed. So when the day ended he was already eleven minutes behind the leader.

During the same 16,42 km long Phalesis special Markko Märtin's Ford Focus, a car noted for its reliability, ran into gearbox problems and he was left with only the first two speeds losing 1m 30s in the process.

Two other favourites also hit trouble in the following special or as in the case of Sébastian Loeb, before it! His faithful co-driver, Daniel Elena, made a right cock up on the liaison stage on the way to the Silyon special. On

his instructions Xsara and driver took a wrong turn and the car ran out of petrol! In fact, he was noting times in his notebook and missed a change in direction. Seven kilometres further on he realised his mistake and told Loeb to double back but the Citroën ground to a halt four kilometres from the refuelling area just before the start of the special. While Elena was at fault his team was also to blame as its fuel calculations left no margin for error so they really shot themselves in the foot! The result was retirement and loss of the championship lead for the Alsatian who, up to then, had done his best to overcome the handicap of being the first to tackle the special. Difficult to find a more stupid reason for retirement.

Petter Solberg in the lead at the end of the second special also went out in no.3 as he was pushing very hard and his Subaru hit a rock damaging it beyond immediate repair.

The season had got off to a bad start for the Norwegian young gun as he had crashed out in Monaco and had not made much of an impression in Sweden.

With Grönholm, Märtin, Loeb and Solberg out of contention it was Harri Rovanpëra who set the pace. He went into the lead at the end of the fourth stage taking advantage of starting from fifteenth spot which gave him a clear run while behind him came a surprising Armin Schwartz. But not for long as the unlucky German was hit with a twenty second penalty due to an over-long exhaust change in the following service park.

The first day ended with the Finn ahead of Mäkinen, Duval and Sainz who had driven a cunning race. He had decided not to let Rovanpërä get too far ahead as well as positioning himself well for the next day,

The Turkish event was very hard on the cars as Mäkinen, Burns, Märtin and Loix found out!

and towards the end of the stage he went pedal to metal in the Xsara climbing from sixth to second in only two specials and conceding just 20.7 secs to the leader. While the Citroën bore the traces of the punishment inflicted on it, it was in perfect working order and ready for the off next day. Duval was third ahead of Makinen while a remarkable Panizzi finished in front of Burns and McRae.

In the second leg Sainz went all out to exploit Rovanperä's vulnerability under pressure. The latter was quickest in the first special of the day but in the second the Spaniard pulled out ten seconds in under thirty kilometres. Rovanpaerä"s reply was all-out attack and he oversteered off into an unyielding rock breaking his 206 WRC's suspension. He crawled to the end of this the tenth stage with a wheel at half-mast and lost six minutes to Carlos! Sainz kept up the pace and in the same special he pulled out some 25 seconds over Panizzi, Märtin and Burns. He also avoided all the traps which caught out Mäkinen (wheel and left-hand front damper broken in special no.8 then wishbone in no.9 followed by power steering and anti-roll bar in no.13), Schwartz (broken rear suspension in no.7) and Loix (two blown turbos in nos 8 and 13 respectively).

So in just one leg the Xsara driver had tightened his stranglehold on the third round of the world championship thanks to his perfectly adapted driving style. He was 1m 19s ahead of Burns, saved by his steadiness, and 1m 44s in front of Duval taking full advantage his Ford Foucus's legendary robustness. Thus in the final leg all Sainz had to do was control his lead. He let McRae, Duval and Grönholm (twice) battle it out for the

A win for Sainz and fourth for McRae. A good result for Citroën.

3

Mâkinen was in second place for a while but in trying to keep up with the Xsaras he gradually destroyed his car.

With his 7th place, Gardemeister takes home two precious points

Panizzi drove a good rally in Turkey (5th). It was some compensation for his Monte Carlo deception.

honour of setting scratch times being content to place himself among the front-runners. The reigning world champion managed to claw his way back up to ninth place scoring a point for Peugeot. Apart from his comeback the overall classification of the rally stayed the same with Carlos going for outright victory and Burns totting up his points like a tight-fisted shop keeper which enabled him to take over the lead in the Drivers World Championship. Duval scored his first rostrum finish fighting off McRae on one of his on-days, the Scot finishing fourth ahead of the Panizzi brothers in fifth. A very happy-and very ambitious young Finn- Kosti Katajamaki gave the VW Polo Junior its first win in the Junior World category even though it had not done specific testing for this rally. Brice Tirabassi, winner of the first round of this competuition in Monte Carlo, went off soon after the start and Daniel Carlsson, who took over the lead, lost all hope when the power assisted steering on his Suzuki broke during the second day. He then crashed out with terminal consequences on the morrow. So Tirabassi left Turkey as joint leader of this category with Katajamaki. Just another fast Finn or a future star?. Only time will tell. ■

Sainz's race craft made all the difference

RECORD
Sainz's 25th

In 1990 Carlos Sainz won the Acropolis Rally and thirteen years later the Turkish one on the other side of the Agean sea. He was the last recruit to join the Citroën team during the 2002-2003 inter season and his victory in Turkey was sweet revenge as he had been left without a drive at the end of 2002 when Ford unceremoniously dropped him. His faithful sponsor MoviStar kept the faith and Guy Fréquelin saw that hiring the talented Spaniard was an opportunity not to be missed even though the Citroën boss was fiercely opposed to the FIA's imposition of a third car. This win created a slightly odd situation in the French firm which had put its money on Colin McRae's fieriness to score victories rather than Sainz's experience as over the last few years the Spaniard seemed to have lost that little extra turn of speed compared with Grönholm or Solberg. But what he lacked in pace he more than made up in steadiness. Always among the front-runners and sometimes victorious as in Turkey this year or Argentina in 2002 (profiting from the Peugeots' disqualification) he took advantage of the numerous setbacks that slowed the quickest drivers as well as Richard Burns's obvious unwillingness to get involed in the battle for victory. After his brilliant third place in Monte Carlo in a new car and team plus a new co-driver-Marc Marti replacing Luis Moya-hewanted to mark his territory in the shortest possible time. Which he did in Turkey perhaps even sooner than he expected! This win helped him to equal the record (25) for the number of victories in the Rally World Championship, held by Colin McRae since the 2002 Acropolis. Thanks to his success and McRae's fourth place (the Scot being the only one of the trio not have scored a win in the Xsara) Citroën was now the sole leader in the Manufacturers Championship as at the end of the Swedish event it had shared this honour with Peugeot. Certainly the Lion squad had been handicapped by Grönholm's misfortune but Citroën too had been hit by the stupid error that led to Loeb running out of petrol. ■

A patient Burns took over second in his 206 that had a trouble-free run.

WRC
FIA WORLD RALLY CHAMPIONSHIP

3rd Leg of the 2003 World Rally Championship for constructors and drivers. **2nd** leg of the Junior WRC championship

Date 26th february to 2nd march 2003

Route
1193,85 km divided in 3 legs
18 special stages on dirt road
(348,71 km).

Superspecial
Thursday 27 february (19h00): Antalya,
1 special (1,54 km)
1st leg
Friday 28th february (08h00-17h30):
Antalya > Kemer > Kemer, 389,55 km;
6 special stages (95,34 km)
2nd leg
Saturday 1th march (06h00-18h24):
Kemer > Kemer, 483,35 km;
7 special stages (158,50 km)
3rd leg
Sunday 2th march (07h00-15h45):
Kemer > Kemer, 320,95 km;
5 special stages (94,87km)

Entry List - Starters - Finishers
70 - 60 - 26

Conditions
hard, dry road

Results — WRC

	Driver/Navigator	Car	Gr.	Times
1	**Sainz - Marti**	Citroën Xsara WRC	A	**4h32'14"1**
2	Burns - Reid	Peugeot 206 WRC		+ 47"9
3	Duval - Fortin	Ford Focus RS WRC 02		+ 1'46"5
4	C. McRae - Ringer	Citroën Xsara WRC		+ 2'09"1
5	Panizzi - Panizzi	Peugeot 206 WRC		+ 2'41"6
6	Märtin - Park	Ford Focus RS WRC 02		+ 3'24"9
7	Gardemeister - Lukander	Skoda Octavia WRC Evo 3		+ 5'01"0
8	Mäkinen - Lindstrom	Subaru Impreza WRC 2003		+7'18"6
9	Grönholm - Rautiainen	Peugeot 206 WRC		+ 10'52"2
10	Loix - Smeets	Hyundai Accent WRC[3]		+ 11'40"4
15	**Katajamäki - Anttila**	**Volkswagen Polo**	Jr.	**+ 36'42"5**

Leading Retirementes (34)

SS13	Rovanperä - Pietiläinen	Peugeot 206 WRC	Rear axle
SS7	Schwarz - Hiemer	Hyundai Accent WRC[3]	Ream suspension
SS6	Auriol - Giraudet	Skoda Octavia WRC Evo 3	Engine
SS4	Hirvonen - Lehtinen	Ford Focus RS WRC 02	Front suspension
SS4	Solberg - Mills	Subaru Impreza WRC 2003	Broken steering
SS3	Loeb - Elena	Citroën Xsara WRC	Out of fuel

TOP ENTRIES

1. Marcus GRÖNHOLM - Timo RAUTIAINEN Peugeot 206 WRC
2. Richard BURNS - Robert REID Peugeot 206 WRC
3. Harri ROVANPERÄ - Risto PIETILÄINEN Peugeot 206 WRC
4. Markko MÄRTIN - Michael PARK Ford Focus RS WRC 02
5. Francois DUVAL - Stéphane PREVOT Ford Focus RS WRC 02
6. Mikko HIRVOVEN - Jamo LEHTINEN Ford Focus RS WRC 02
7. Petter SOLBERG - Philip MILLS Subaru Impreza WRC 2003
8. Tommi MÄKINEN - Kaj LINDSTROM Subaru Impreza WRC 2003
10. Armin SCHWARZ - Manfred HIEMER Hyundai Accent WRC[3]
11. Freddy LOIX- Sven SMEETS Hyundai Accent WRC[3]
14. Didier AURIOL - Denis GIRAUDET Skoda Octavia WRC Evo 3
15. Toni GARDEMEISTER - Paavo LUKANDER Skoda Octavia WRC Evo 3
17. Colin McRAE- Derek RINGER Citroën Xsara WRC
18. Sébastien LOEB - Daniel ELENA Citroën Xsara WRC
19. Carlos SAINZ - Marc MARTI Citroën Xsara WRC
21. Gilles PANIZZI - Hervé PANIZZI Peugeot 206 WRC
22. Juuso PYKÄLISTÖ - Esko MERTSALMI Peugeot 206 WRC
24. Balazs BENIK - Bence RACE Ford Focus WRC RS 01
51. Mirco BALDACCI - Giovanni BERNACCHINI Fiat Punto
52. Daniel CARLSSON - Mattias ANDERSON Suzuki Ignis
54. Kosti KATAJAMAKI - Miikka ANTTILA Volkswagen Polo
57. Dimitar ILIEV - Peter SIVOV Peugeot 206
58. Marcos LIGATO - Ruben GARGIA Fiat Punto
59. Beppo HARRACH - Michael KOLBACH Ford Puma
61. Brice TIRABASSI - Jacques-Julien RENUCCI Renault Clio
63. Massimo CECCATO- Mitia DOTTA Fiat Punto
64. Ville-Pertti TEURONEN - Harri KAAPRO Suzuki Ignis
65. Abdo FEGHALI - Joseph MATAR Ford Puma
67. Alessandro BROCCOLI - Simona GIRELLI Opel Corsa
68. Juraj SEBALJ - Toni KLINC Renault Clio
69. Salvador CANELLAS - Xavier AMIGO Suzuki Ignis
70. Guy WILKS - Phil PUGH Ford Puma
71. Urmo AAVA - Kuldar SIKK Suzuki Ignis
101. Simon JEAN JOSEPH - Jack BOYERE Renault Clio

Special Stage Times

SS1 Efes Pilsen (1,54 km)
1.Grönholm 1'12"1; 2.Solberg +0"1;
3.Burns +0"2; 4.C. McRae/Sainz +0"3;
6.Märtin +0"5; 7.Mäkinen/Loeb +0"7...
Jr. (24) Tirabassi +10"7

SS2 Simena I (2,73 km)
1.Rovanperä/Solberg 1'52"7;
3.Pykälistö +0"8; 4.Panizzi +1"4;
5.Hirvonen +1"5; 6.Märtin/Sainz +1"6;
8.Mäkinen +1"7...
Jr. (21) Carlsson +14"6

SS3 Phaselis I (16,42 km)
1.Solberg 12'28"6; 2.Mäkinen +7"0;
3.Duval +7"7; 4.Schwarz +9"7;
5.C. McRae +11"9; 6.Rovanperä +13"1;
7.Sainz +14"8; 8.Panizzi +15"7...
Jr. (18) Carlsson +1'38"5

SS4 Silyon I (29,87 km)
1.Rovanperä 23'51"8; 2.Schwarz +7"8;
3.Sainz +10"8; 4.Panizzi +12"2;
5.Mäkinen +18"7; 6.Duval +18"9;
7.Loix +24"2; 8.Burns +24"4...
Jr (16) Carlsson +2'32"0

SS5 Perge I (14,91 km)
1.Märtin 11'50"5; 2.Rovanperä +0"8;
3.Duval +1"3; 4.Panizzi +1"9;
5.Loix +3"3; 6.Mäkinen +4"0;
7.Burns +5"8; 8.Sainz +7"1...
Jr (15) Carlsson +53"5

SS6 Silyon II (29,87 km)
1.Rovanperä 23'19"1; 2.Märtin +0"6;
3.Sainz +1"8; 4.Duval +13"7;
5. Mäkinen +15"0; 6.Burns +16"1;
7.Panizzi +20"0; 8.Auriol +23"6...
Jr. (18) Ligato +3'06"2

SS7 Olympos I (20,44 km)
1.Rovanperä 16'45"1; 2.Duval +3"4;
3.Mäkinen +8"9; 4.Burns +9"4;
5. C. McRae +10"2; 6.Sainz +11"4;
7.Grönholm +12"3; 8.Märtin +13"2...
Jr. (17) Ligato +2'24"3

SS8 Kulmluca I (28,92 km)
1.Sainz 24'47"0; 2.Burns +2"6;
3.Märtin +9"4; 4.Rovanperä +10"0;
5.Grönholm +10"5; 6.Mäkinen +18"0;
7.Panizzi +20"2; 8.C. McRae +22"6...
Jr. (17) Teuronen +2'48"9

SS9 Phaselis II (15,48 km)
1.Grönholm 11'51"4; 2.Mäkinen +2"2;
3.Rovanperä +3"8; 4.Sainz +4"5;
5.Burns +5"0; 6.C. McRae +7"4;
7.Märtin +10"5; 8.Duval +11"2...
Jr. (17) Carlsson +1'38"0

SS10 Myra I (24,01 km)
1.Sainz 21'45"4; 2.Panizzi +24"9;
3.Märtin +25"3; 4.Burns +25"7;
5.Duval +30"8; 6.Grönholm +33"4;
7.Gardemeister +34"8; 8.C. McRae +40"6...
Jr. (15) Carlsson +2'30"6

SS11 Kemer I (20,29 km)
1.Burns 15'06"8; 2.C. McRae +0"9;
3.Grönholm +4"6; 4.Sainz +6"3;
5.Märtin +10"1; 6.Duval +10"9;
7.Gardemeister +20"5; 8.Loix +30"4...
Jr. (13) Carlsson +1'34"4

SS12 Olympos II (20,44 km)
1.Märtin 16'29"6; 2.Duval +2"5;
3.Sainz +4"1; 4.Gardemeister +8"1;
5.C. McRae +10"2; 6.Panizzi +11"3;
7.Burns +13"4; 8.Mäkinen +13"6...
Jr. (16) Teuronen +2'05"3

SS13 Kumluca II (28,92 km)
1.Sainz 24'27"1; 2.Grönholm +5"3;
3.Märtin +9"1; 4.Burns +13"9;
5.Panizzi +26"8; 6.Gardemeister+30"6;
7.Duval +34"2; 8.C. McRae +37"8...
Jr. (14) Teuronen +3'12"6

SS14 Simena II (13,39 km)
1.C. McRae 1'51"3; 2.Märtin +0"1;
3.Burns +0"7; 4.Sainz +0"8;
5.Grönholm +0"9; 6.Panizzi +1"6;
7.Duval +1"9; 8.Loix +2"0...
Jr. (15) Carlsson +14"6

SS15 Myra II (24,01 km)
1.Burns 21'20"7; 2.Grönholm +4"3;
3.Märtin +4"9; 4.Sainz +10"6;
5.Mäkinen +12"3; 6.Panizzi +12"3;
7.C. McRae +16"4; 8.Duval +25"5...
Jr. (13) Katajamäki +2'29§"8

SS16 Arykanda (12,00 km)
1.Duval 8'13"4; 2.Märtin +0"4;
3.C. McRae +4"6; 4.Burns +4"5;
5.Grönholm +4"8; 6.Sainz +4"9;
7.Panizzi +7"9; 8.Mäkinen +11"4...
Jr. (16) Wilks +1'05"9

SS17 Perge II (24,97 km)
1.Grönholm 18'13"8; 2.Burns +10"2;
3.Märtin +10"3; 4.Sainz +13"4;
5.Panizzi +14"0; 6.C. McRae +15"1;
7.Duval +17"0; 8.Mäkinen +25"2...
Jr. (13) Katajamäki +2'41"2

SS18 Kemer II (20,50 km)
1.Grönholm 14'46"5; 2.C. McRae +9"6;
3.Burns +11"5; 4.Märtin +13"4;
5.Duval +16"6; 6.Panizzi +19"2;
7.Mäkinen +24"5; 8.Sainz +28"8...
Jr. (15) Katajamäki +2'37"7

Championship Classifications

FIA Drivers (3/14)
1.Burns 18; 2.C. McRae 17; 3.Sainz 16; 4.Märtin 13; 5.Loeb 12;
6.Grönholm 10; 7.Mäkinen 9; 8.Duval 8; 9.Panizzi 4;
10.Gardemeister 3; 11.Solberg 3; 12.Robert 3; 13.Schwarz 1

FIA Constructors (3/14)
1.Citroën 39; 2.Peugeot 31; 3.Ford 25; 4.Subaru 13; 5.Skoda 6;
6.Hyundai 3

FIA Junior WRC (2/7)
1.Katajamäki 10; 2.Tirabassi 10; 3.Canellas 8; 4.Ligato 8; 5.Broccoli 6;
6.Wilks 6; 7.Aava 5; 8.Teuronen 5; 9.Ceccato 4; 10.Cecchettini 4;
11.Feghali 3; 12.Sebalj 3; 13.Baldacci 2; 14.Iliev 2; 15.Harrach 1

FIA Production Car WRC (1/7)
1.Blomqvist 10; 2.Singh 8; 3.Rowe 6; 4.Bourne 5; 5.Holowczyc 4;
6.Roman 3; 7.Sztuka 2; 8.Richard 1

Performers

	1	2	3	4	5	6
Grönholm	4	2	1	-	3	1
Rovanperä	4	1	1	1	-	1
Sainz	3	-	3	6	-	2
Märtin	2	3	5	1	1	2
Burns	2	2	3	4	1	
Solberg	2	1	-	-	-	-
Duval	1	2	2	1	2	2
C. McRae	1	2	1	1	3	2
Mäkinen	-	2	1	-	3	2
Panizzi	-	1	-	3	2	4
Schwarz	-	1	-	1	-	-
Pykälistö	-	1	-	-	-	-
Gardemeister	-	-	-	1	-	1
Loix	-	-	-	-	1	-
Hirvonen	-	-	-	-	1	-

Event Leaders

SS1	Grönholm
SS2 >SS3	Solberg
SS4 > SS9	Rovanperä
SS10 > SS18	Sainz

Kosti Katajamäki

The Octavias were at home on New Zealand soil. Gardemeister, 5th, showed a fine turn of speed.

The new Subaru engine pleased Araï, winner of the Group N category in his Impreza.

THE FINE
Mäkinen caught by the cops!

In the 90s Tommi Mäkinen was the best rally driver in the world (maybe the greatest ever) but since his arrival at Subaru at the beginning of 2002 he seemed to have lost all his panache. As the rallies unfolded he found it increasingly difficult to match his former exploits. Yet he thought that the 2003 version of the new Subaru Impreza WRC would allow him to repeat some of his former glorious exploits. It was not to be as Petter Solbergh outpaced him more often than not in the same car. In New Zealand he was the centre of an amazing mix up. At the end of the first leg he was seventh and asked his crew to swap the central differential for a new one in the first service halt on the second day. The engineers and mechanics wanted to do the job right and decided to change the suspension as well. Unfortunately, they were delayed by a jammed bolt and repairs dragged on. When Mäkinen finally got back in the car he was furious and sped off to the checkpoint but was blocked by a badly parked van, one belonging to his own team! He finally got past and set off flat out on the liaison section. And that is something one must never do in New Zealand (nor indeed in his home country)! A local police radar timed him at 102 km/h in a built up area. So what happened next was inevitable: chase, arrest, discussions to prevent him having his licence confiscated, a fine and the Subaru at last set off for the

tenth special. And that was not the end of the story! On the basis of a report sent in by a zealous policeman to the organisers the latter decided to inflict a penalty of 200 dollars per kilometre over the speed limit, which came to 9800 dollars. But there was more to come for the Finn. Judging that Mäkinen had refused to obey the police-he should have stopped in the first convenient place following his control, which he didn't-race control docked him five minutes for two road infringements. This explained his seventh place some

9m 50.2s behind the winner. However, Subaru did not leave Kiwi land empty-handed as Araï-Sircombe won the Group N category, the FIA Production one, led after two rounds by the trio Blomqvist, Singh-the reigning champion not very happy with his Proton which was at the end of the road-and Rowe all dead-heating with eleven points. The new Group N Impreza also made a big impression in this rally and the Japanese car won the category easily from the Argentinean Ligato in his Mitsubishi. ∎

Tommi Mäkinen's brush with the law eclipsed his race performance.

D.G.+K.M. TANNER

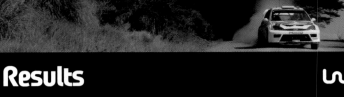

Results WRC

	Driver/Navigator	Car	Gr.	Time
1	**Grönholm - Rautiainen**	Peugeot 206 WRC	A	3h45'21"2
2	Burns - Reid	Peugeot 206 WRC		+1'08"7
3	Solberg - Mills	Subaru Impreza WRC 2003		+2'09"8
4	Loeb - Elena	Citroën Xsara WRC		+ 4'15"4
5	Gardemeister - Lukander	Skoda Octavia WRC Evo 3		+ 8'13"8
6	A. McRae - Senior	Mitsubishi Lancer WRC 02		+ 9'14"2
7	Mäkinen - Lindstrom	Subaru Impreza WRC 2003		+ 9'50"2
8	Auriol - Giraudet	Skoda Octavia WRC Evo 3		+10'08"6
9	Duval - Prévot	Ford Focus RS WRC 03		+ 11'11"7
10	Hirvonen - Lehtinen	Ford Focus RS WRC 02		+ 13'42"3
11	**Arai - Sircombe**	**Subaru Impreza WRX**	Prod.	+ 18'09"1

Leading Retirementes (34)

SS18	Loix - Smeets	Hyundai Accent WRC³	Accident
SS14	Rovanperä - Pietiläinen	Peugeot 206 WRC	Accident
SS14	Märtin - Park	Ford Focus RS WRC 03	Engine
SS7	Välimäki - Gardemeister	Hyundai Accent WRC³	Accident
SS6	C. McRae - Ringer	Citroën Xsara WRC	Accident
SS1	Schwarz - Hiemer	Hyundai Accent WRC³	Accident

4th Leg of the 2003 World Rally Championship for constructors and drivers. 2nd Leg of FIA Production Car WRC Championship.

Date 10th to 13th april 2003

Route
1299 km divided in 3 legs
22 special stages on dirt roads
(403,24 km)

1st leg
Friday 11th april (07h00-17h00):
Auckland > Paparoa, 388 km;
9 special stages (139,05 km)
2nd leg
Saturday 12th april (08h30-20h20):
Paparoa > Auckland, 456 km;
7 special stages (150,39 km)
3rd leg
Sunday 13th april (06h00-15h30):
Te Kauwhata > Auckland, 455 km;
6 special stages (113,80 km)

Entry List - Starters - Finishers
86 - 80 - 46

Conditions
rain for the first day, dry on the second day and humid roads for the Sunday.

TOP ENTRIES

1 Marcus GRÖNHOLM - Timo RAUTIAINEN Peugeot 206 WRC
2 Richard BURNS - Robert REID Peugeot 206 WRC
3 Harri ROVANPERÄ - Risto PIETILÄINEN Peugeot 206 WRC
4 Markko MÄRTIN - Michael PARK Ford Focus RS WRC 03
5 Francois DUVAL - Stéphane PREVOT Ford Focus RS WRC 03
6 Mikko HIRVOVEN - Jamo LEHTINEN Ford Focus RS WRC 02
7 Petter SOLBERG - Philip MILLS Subaru Impreza WRC 2003
8 Tommi MÄKINEN - Kaj LINDSTROM Subaru Impreza WRC 2003
10 Armin SCHWARZ - Manfred HIEMER Hyundai Accent WRC³
11 Freddy LOIX- Sven SMEETS Hyundai Accent WRC³
12 Jussi VÄLIMÄKI - Tero GARDEMEISTER Hyundai Accent WRC³
14 Didier AURIOL - Denis GIRAUDET Skoda Octavia WRC Evo 3
15 Toni GARDEMEISTER - Paavo LUKANDER Skoda Octavia WRC Evo 3
17 Colin McRAE- Derek RINGER Citroën Xsara WRC
18 Sébastien LOEB - Daniel ELENA Citroën Xsara WRC
19 Carlos SAINZ - Marc MARTI Citroën Xsara WRC
20 Antony WARMBOLD - Gemma PRICE Ford Focus 2001
32 Alister MCRAE - David SENIOR Mitsubishi Lancer WRC 02
33 Kristian SOHLBERG - Jakke HONKANEN Mitsubishi Lancer WRC 02
34 Tomasz KUCHAR - Maciej SZCEPANIAK Ford Focus RS WRC 02
35 Manfred STOHL - Ika MINOR Peugeut 206 WRC
51 Karamjit SINGH - Allen OH Potron Pert
52 Daniel SOLA - Alex ROMANI Mitsubishi Carisma GT EVO 4
53 Ramon FERREYROS - Javier MARIN Mitsubishi Lancer Evo VI
54 Toshihiro ARAI - Tony SIRCOMBE Subaru Impreza WRX
55 Martin ROWE - Trevor AGNEW Subaru Impreza
57 Giovanni MANFRINATO - Claudio CONDOTTA Mitsubishi Lancer Evo
58 Marcos LIGATO - Ruben GARGIA Mitsubishi Lancer Evo VII
60 Nial MCSHEA - Chris PATTERSON Mitsubishi Lancer Evo VI
62 Possum BOURNE - Mark STACEY Subaru Impreza
64 Joakim ROMAN - Tina MITAKIDOU Mitsubishi Lancer Evo V
65 Stig BLOMQVIST - Ana GONI Subaru Impreza
66 Hamed AL WAHAIBI - Nick BEACH Mitsubishi Lancer Evo
67 Krzysztof HOLOWCZYC - Lurasz KURZEJA Mitsubishi Lancer Evo VI

Special Stage Times

SS1 Batley I (19,81 km)
1.Grönholm 10'45"2; 2.Märtin +6"1;
3.Rovanperä +9"2; 4.Solberg +9"7;
5.Burns +15"9; 6.Stohl +16"1;
7.Mäkinen +17"5; 8.Sainz +20"6...
FIA Prod. (23) Arai +59"5

SS2 Waipu Gorge I (11,23 km)
1.Burns 6'37"0; 2. Märtin +0"7;
3.Grönholm +0"9; 4.Solberg +2"7;
5.Mäkinen +6"6; 6.Sainz +8"2;
7.Rovanperä +8"4; 8.Auriol +9"1...
FIA Prod. (19) Al Wahaibi +30"7

SS3 Brooks I (16,03 km)
1.Grönholm 9'46"3; 2.Solberg +5"1;
3.Rovanperä +6"6; 4.Märtin/Loeb +7"5;
6.Burns +7"8; 7.Mäkinen +8"9;
8.Stohl +10"2...
FIA Prod. (22) Arai +45"2

SS4 New Cassidy (21,63 km)
1.Grönholm 12'13"7; 2.Rovanperä +1"5;
3.Solberg +2"9; 4.Sohlberg +4"4;
5.Märtin +5"0; 6.Mäkinen +6"8;
7.Loeb +11"2; 8.Stohl +13"0...
FIA Prod. (23) Bourne +49"9

SS5 Paparoa Station I (11,64 km)
1.Grönholm 6'18"2; 2.C. McRae +1"5;
3.Burns +1"7; 4.Solberg +2"9;
5.Märtin +3"3; 6.Mäkinen +5"9;
7.Loeb/Sainz +6"6...
FIA Prod. (24) Arai +30"8

SS6 Batley II (19,81 km)
1.Grönholm 10'33"0; 2.Märtin +2"9;
3.Rovanperä +4"5; 4.Burns +8"2;

5.Loeb +8"4; 6.Solberg +8"5;
7.Stohl +10"8; 8.Sohlberg +12"1...
FIA Prod. (20) Ferreyros +53"1

SS7 Waipu Gorge II (11,23 km)
1.Burns 6'34"9; 2.Grönholm +1"7;
3.Märtin +2"2; 4.Loeb +3"8;
5.Solberg +3"9; 6.Sainz +4"5;
7.Mäkinen +6"1; 8.Auriol +9"7...
FIA Prod. (19) Arai +35"4

SS8 Brooks II (16,03 km)
1.Grönholm 9'22"9; 2.Burns +6"6;
3.Solberg +7"9; 4.Loeb +8"8;
5.Rovanperä +10"0; 6.Märtin +10"3;
7.Stohl +13"8; 8.Sainz +14"1...
FIA Prod. (21) Ferreyros +48"7

SS9 Paparoa Station II (11,64 km)
1.Grönholm 6'11"7; 2.Burns +0"8;
3.Solberg +2"6; 4.Märtin +2"7;
5.Loeb +4"1; 6.Sainz +6"9;
7.Rovanperä +7"2; 8.Stohl +8"2...
FIA Prod. (17) Ferreyros +27"9

SS10 Parahi/Ararua (59,00 km)
1.Grönholm 33'20"5; 2.Burns +10"5;
3.Rovanperä +20"6; 4.Märtin +24"3;
5.Loeb +33"9; 6.Solberg +37"5;
7.Mäkinen +1'05"6;
8.Gardemeister +1'11"2...
FIA Prod. (15) Arai +2'31"9

SS11 Mititai Finish (20,14 km)
1.Märtin 10'03"0; 2.Grönholm +0"7;
3.Rovanperä +9"5; 4.Burns +11"1;
5.Solberg +11"5; 6.Loeb +18"7;
7.Sainz +21"2; 8.Mäkinen +24"8...
FIA Prod. (20) Al Wahaibi +1'03"8

SS12 Tokatoka (10,14 km)
1.Märtin 5'07"1; 2.Grönholm +0"5;
3.Burns +2"5; 4.Rovanperä +4"1;
5.Solberg +5"7; 6.Loeb +7"5;
7.Sainz +8"3; 8.Sohlberg +9"0...
FIA Prod. (16) McShea +27"0

SS13 Parahi (25,18 km)
1.Märtin 12'42"6; 2.Burns +3"0;
3.Rovanperä +6"5; 4.Loeb +9"7;
5.Sainz +13"5; 6.Mäkinen +17"6;
7.Sohlberg +18"0; 8.Gardemeister +25"2...
FIA Prod. (17) Arai +1'07"4

SS14 Ararua (31,75 km)
1.Grönholm 19'01"3; 2.Burns +16"6;
3.Loeb +19"4; 4.Solberg +21"4;
5.Mäkinen +27"7; 6.Sainz +32"4;
7.Auriol +52"8; 8.Loix +1'02"2...
FIA Prod. (12=) Singh +2'01"7

SS15 Manukau Super I (2,09 km)
1.Duval 1'36"4; 2.(FIA Prod) Arai/
Ligato +1"3; 4.Loix/Herbert +1"8;
6.Mäkinen +2"0; 7.Crocker +2"7;
8.Sainz +4"2...

SS16 Manukau Super II (2,09 km)
1.Solberg 1'40"2; 2.Loix +1"6; 3.Sainz/
A. McRae +1"8; 5.Mäkinen +2"0;
6.Grönholm +2"1; 7.Burns +2"8;
8.Auriol +3"0...
FIA Prod. (17) Singh +10"5

SS17 Te Akau South Reserv (27,34 km)
1.Grönholm 15'49"7; 2.Solberg +4"5;
3.Burns +12"8; 4.Loeb +18"4;
5.Gardemeister +31"6; 6.Mäkinen +32"9;

7.Sainz +33"4; 8.Auriol +38"2...
FIA Prod. (13) Sola +1'12"2

SS18 Te Akau North (32,26 km)
1.Burns 17'43"0; 2.Grönholm +0"2;
3.Sohlberg +2"1; 4.Märtin +29"6;
5.Auriol +31"5; 6.Gardemeister +31"6;
7.Sainz +36"1; 8.A. McRae +43"9...
FIA Prod. (13) Sola +1'07"6

SS19 Ridge/Campbell (16,45 km)
1.Burns 8'53"7; 2.Grönholm +0"6;
3.Solberg +1"8; 4.Mäkinen +10"4;
5.Loeb +11"6; 6.Gardemeister +13"4;
7.Sainz +16"2; 8.Auriol +18"6...
FIA Prod. (12) Arai +41"1

SS20 Ridge/Campbell II (16,45 km)
1.Burns 8'46"9; 2.Grönholm +1"4;
3.Solberg +2"2; 4.Loeb +6"3;
5.Mäkinen +6"9; 6.Gardemeister +8"8;
7.Auriol +10"9; 8.Duval +15"8...
FIA Prod. (13) Arai +46"7

SS21 Flyfe (10,60 km)
1.Burns 5'42"3; 2.Grönholm +0"7;
3.Loeb +5"2; 4.Mäkinen +7"5;
5.Auriol +7"9; 6.Solberg +9"6;
7.Sainz +10"4; 8.Gardemeister +11"5...
FIA Prod. (14=) Al Wahaibi +25"0

SS22 Flyfe II (10,60 km)
1.Burns 5'36"9; 2.Grönholm +2"1;
3.Solberg +3"9; 4.Loeb +5"3;
5.Mäkinen +5"5; 6.Sainz +7"5;
7.Duval +7"8; 8.Gardemeister +8"4...
FIA Prod. (12) Sola +25"9

Championship Classifications

FIA Drivers (4/14)
1.Burns 26; 2.Grönholm 20; 3.Loeb 17; 4.C. McRae 17; 5.Sainz 16;
6.Märtin 13; 7.Mäkinen 11; 8.Solberg 9; 9.Duval 8; 10.Gardemeister 7;
11.Panizzi 4; 12.Robert 3; 13.A. McRae 3; 14.Schwarz 1; 15.Auriol 1

FIA Constructors (4/14)
1.Peugeot 49; 2.Citroën 44; 3.Ford 26; 4.Subaru 22; 5.Skoda 12;
6.Hyundai 3

FIA Junior WRC (2/7)
1.Katajamäki 10; 2.Tirabassi 10; 3.Canellas 8; 4.Ligato 8; 5.Broccoli 6;
6.Wilks 6; 7.Aava 5; 8.Teuronen 5; 9.Ceccato 4; 10.Cecchettini 4;
11.Feghali 3; 12.Sebalj 3; 13.Baldacci 2; 14.Iliev 2; 15.Harrach 1

FIA Production Car WRC (2/7)
1.Blomqvist 11; 2.Singh 11; 3.Rowe 11; 4.Arai 10; 5.Ligato 8;
6.Al Wahaibi 6; 7.Bourne 5; 8.Ferreyros 4; 9.Holowczyc 4; 10.Roman 3;
11.McShea 2; 12.Sztuka 2; 13.Richard 1

Performers

	1	2	3	4	5	6
Grönholm	10	8	1	-	-	1
Burns	7	5	3	2	1	1
Märtin	3	3	1	3	2	1
Solberg	1	2	7	4	3	3
Duval	1	-	-	-	-	-
Rovanperä	-	1	6	1	1	-
Loix	-	1	-	1	-	-
C. McRae	-	1	-	-	-	-
Ligato	-	1	-	-	-	-
Arai	-	1	-	-	-	-
Loeb	-	-	1	7	4	2
Sainz	-	1	-	1	5	-
A. McRae	-	-	1	-	-	-
Mäkinen	-	-	-	3	5	5
Sohlberg	-	-	-	1	-	-
Hebert	-	-	-	1	-	-
Auriol	-	-	-	-	2	-
Gardemeister	-	-	-	-	1	3
Stohl	-	-	-	-	-	1

Event Leaders

SS1 > SS22   Grönholm

Kristian Sohlberg

Previous winners

1977	Bacchelli - Rosetti Fiat 131 Abarth	1993	McRae - Ringer Subaru Legacy RS
1978	Brookes - Porter Ford Escort RS	1994	McRae - Ringer Subaru Impreza
1979	Mikkola - Hertz Ford Escort RS	1995	McRae - Ringer Subaru Impreza
1980	Salonen - Harjanne Datsun 160J	1996	Burns - Reid Mitsubishi Lancer Ev.3
1982	Waldegaard - Thorzelius Toyota Celica GT	1997	Eriksson - Parmander Subaru Impreza WRC
1983	Rohrl - Geistdorfer Opel Ascona 400	1998	Sainz - Moya Toyota Corolla WRC
1984	Blomqvist - Cederberg Audi Quattro A2	1999	Mäkinen - Mannisenmäki Mitsubishi Lancer Evo 6
1985	Salonen - Harjanne Peugeot 205 T16	2000	Grönholm - Rautiainen Peugeot 206 WRC
1986	Kankkunen - Piironen Peugeot 205 T16	2001	Grönholm - Rautiainen Peugeot 206 WRC
1987	Wittmann - Patermann Lancia Delta HF 4WD	2002	Grönholm - Rautiainen Peugeot 206 WRC
1988	Haider - Hinterleitner Opel Kadett GSI		
1989	Carlsson - Carlsson Mazda 323 Turbo		
1990	Sainz - Moya Toyota Celica GT-Four		
1991	Sainz - Moya Toyota Celica GT-Four		
1992	Sainz - Moya Toyota Celica Turbo 4WD		

Argentina

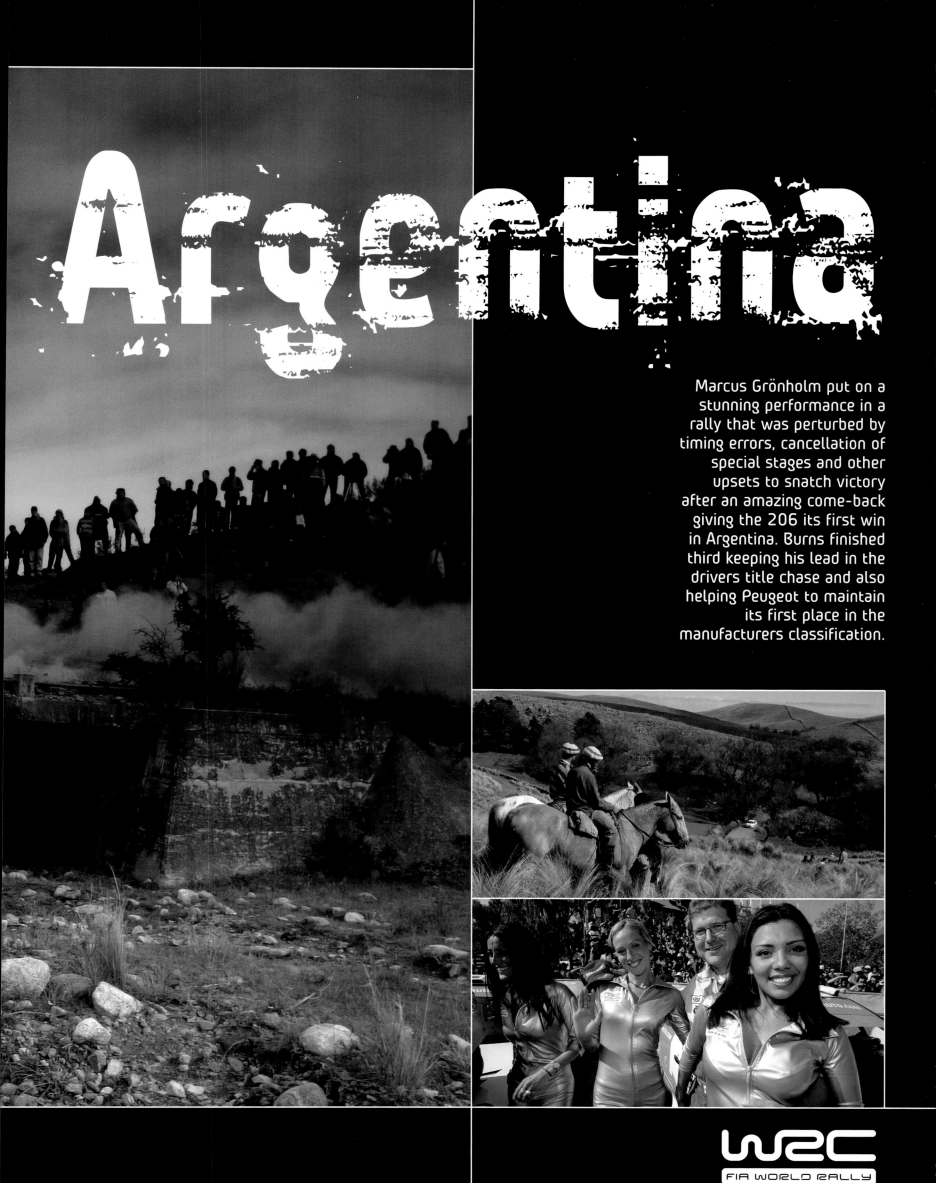

Argentina

Marcus Grönholm put on a stunning performance in a rally that was perturbed by timing errors, cancellation of special stages and other upsets to snatch victory after an amazing come-back giving the 206 its first win in Argentina. Burns finished third keeping his lead in the drivers title chase and also helping Peugeot to maintain its first place in the manufacturers classification.

WRC
FIA WORLD RALLY
CHAMPIONSHIP

Grönholm's drive despite the time keeping problems was quite simply mind-boggling.

Lost in his thoughts, Sainz could have established a new record for victories without a small misunderstanding.

Mäkinen did some on the spot testing when his gearbox cried enough.

THE RALLY
Marcus' stunning drive!

After the two super specials organised as curtain raisers and won by Grönholm and Burns respectively, the serious business began. Marcus Grönholm was head and shoulders above his rivals and showed the same brilliant form as in New Zealand. The first to to pose a threat to the Finn was Tommi Mäkinen whose Pirelli-shod Subaru has always been at home on the South American routes. His moment of glory was brief as his gearbox started to play up and then blocked during the second stage of the day. Nevertheless he was up to second place by the end of the fifth special just when the timing went

askew. Grönholm was beside himself with rage in the service park that closed the first round on Friday and there was no calming the reigning world champion. The times given by the official timekeepers bore no relation to those of his co-driver Timo Rautiäinen. The latter is not only a stickler for accuracy but also a computer analyst as skilled at manipulating figures as his driver is behind the steering wheel. And that's saying something! The mistakes were enormous, between ten and thirteen seconds, and the classifications either totally wrong or non-exisent. Certain drivers like the Peugeot team leader were heavily

penalised on the time sheets for the sixth special while others like Loeb and Mäkinen were given the right times. Finally 13 seconds were added to their times exactly the handicap imposed on Grönholm by the time keepers. In the following special he was penalised no fewer than twenty seconds!

At the end of the first leg Nicola Gullino, the new Peugeot team manager replacing François Chatriot gone to Citroën, justified not only his appointment but also his reputation as a master of the regulations and procedures. The cunning Italian enabled the Stewards to prove Grönholm right

François Duval applied himself to learning a layout with which he was not familiar.

Auriol had a difficult rally as he was suffering from an injured right wrist due to steering wheel whiplash

after watching the in-car footage taken in the Peugeot. But this decision was announced at the end of the day and not during it which did nothing for the peace of mind of the crew in the no.1 Peugeot. After the errors in stages six and seven Marcus set off like a scalded cat and began to overdrive. In the famous Aschochinga section four kilometres after the start he made a mistake and destroyed the rear suspension on his car finishing the special on three wheels. "I was obsessed by those twenty seconds," he later admitted. However his error cost him 1m 50s and the lead and he fell back to sixth place. Carlos Sainz, who had been running in second spot following the problems that hit Makinen's Subaru, (Solberg seemed out to destroy the other Impreza as he overturned the car, visited the scenery and spun), found himself handed the

rally lead on a plate. And when Carlos is in front he is as difficult to dislodge as a tick in a dog's ear! At the end of the first stage the Spaniard was 22.4 secs in front of Markko Märtin slowed by gearbox problems and 40.1 secs ahead of the anonymous Richard Burns. Back in sixth Marcus Grönholm was 1m 4.3s behind but for the big man from Espoo this was not an insurmountable handicap.

On Saturday morning he set off with the bit between his teeth, more determined than ever. The day's programme consisted of three stages around the village of San Marcos Sierra to be covered twice. In the past the Argentinians were reproached for their rash behaviour along the specials but laterly they have begun to respect instructions and keep a weather eye open. This weekend they were very

Rovanperä was briefly second before falling back due to punctures.

In Argentina the multitudes of enthusiastic spectators upset the organisation a little.

The new Focus
helped Märtin to
really shine

Harri Rovanperä
made the gauchos
very happy!

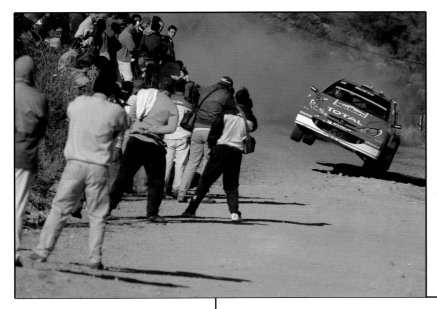

disciplined and yet the very first special of the day was cancelled as after the first three cars (Hiroven, Gardemeister and Mäkinen) had gone through the FIA safety delegate stated that the service crews was too big and badly placed. The drivers were gob-smacked when they learnt of the cancellation. According to them there was no reason to do this. And so what did the spectators do as soon as they heard of the cancellation, they went to the next one which was just a stone's throw away. Around the no.15 special the crowd was even denser than it had been for no.14. The first cars set off

followed by Marcus Grönholm who set an incredible time pulling back almost a second per kilometre on Solberg and Mäkinen in their Subarus. At the finish Marcus again couldn't believe his ears, another cancellation. The tall Finn went completely ballistic and made no bones about saying what he thought. "We drive like crazy for nothing," he shouted. In addition, his incredible time was used as a set time for the five drivers ahead of him in the classification. What was even more serious was that he had really driven the hell out of his tyres which he had to use in the next stage and had not spared his car either. This was not the case for the others so where was any idea of justice in all this?

But this mind-boggling day was not yet over. Following the second cancellation the spectators thought; 'Well it can't happen again' as they walked to the third stage whose start had been delayed by almost two hours. In this one and the next Grönholm driving in a state of cold fury set two scratch times and climbed up to fourth place. He then went home to bed like his rivals because the organisers decided not to run the final two specials which were very dusty at night and could have been dangerous. They modified the programme to reschedule them for next day showing remarkable proof of improvisation as marshals, volunteers and police had to be mobilised two hours earlier than foreseen!

Thus on Sunday 11th May 2003 seven specials had to be covered and everybody was asking themselves the same question: could Grönholm get back among the leaders and fight for victory? In the latter's mind there was no doubt. His task was made easier by the penalty inflicted on Carlos Sainz (see below) right from the outset which dropped the Spaniard back to third place. So who was left in front of him? Richard Burns, no problem, Markko Martin, a tougher nut to crack as the Estonian in his new Focus had had a fantastic rally up to then. He was now in the lead following Sainz's penalty and it would not be easy to catch him. The intensity of the forthcoming battle almost hid the fact that there were

Acropolis

Markko Märtin finally scored his first world championship victory thanks to his skilled driving and the speed and solidity of his Ford Focus. It was a well-deserved success for the Estonian in what was only the third time out for the new blue oval challenger. Burns drove his usual cautious race finishing fourth and hanging on to the Driver Championship lead.

THE RALLY
Markko Superstar!

Markko Märtin's first win was a long time in coming and was a reward for his patience and talent. Surprisingly enough at the start of the sixth round of the world championship the Estonian-British pairing of Märtin-Park in their Ford Focus was favourite. This seemed a bit of a contradiction as neither car nor driver had yet won a race and the Ford, still in its infancy, had not shown bulletproof reliability, and it was competing in a rally generally recognised as being one of the toughest on the machines. However, there were others who bet on the Marcus Grönholm/Peugeot tandem even if the Finn had never really shone on Greek gravel.

So why was Martin the bookies' favourite? Because of the promise shown the previous year in the third works Ford and the amazing potential of the new Focus WRC03 which seemed to have been considerably beefed up for the Greek event. Christian Loriaux, the man who designed the car in only seven months said on the eve of the start: "We've done a lot of work on the road holding in the quick sections while keeping the Ford's strong point, its solidity in the gruelling ones." Since 1999 the Focus has won three Acropolis rallies, two Safaris and two in Cyprus a total of seven victories in the toughest events on the calendar out of the eleven scored by the make. Would the Belgian's predictions be borne out? Only time would tell!

Märtin did not go into the lead straight away as it was his young, daredevil team-mate François Duval with the experienced Stéphane Prévot (formerly with Bruno Thiery) as co-driver since the start of 2003, who hit the front. However, the big news

It was Duval's first Acropolis in WRC and for a time he matched the pace of his team leader.

Burns' race was spoilt by gearbox problems.

Rovanperä tried to stay with Märtin but his 206 was not reliable enough.

of the start of the first leg was not Duval's performance but Sébastien Loeb's retirement. Eleven kilometres after the start from Pavliani the Xsara's engine stopped dead. "The temperature went up to 130°," said the driver afterwards, "and I felt the engine tightening up. Then it just stopped." It was a big blow to the Frenchman as he lost out in the world championship falling back three places to seventh. In addition, he was eliminated from one of the first rallies on gravel in which he hoped to shine. Armin Schwartz's Hyundaï also gave up the ghost not far from the Xsara (broken alternator belt), these two being the first retirements among the works teams. Freddy Loix almost joined them as his Accent caught fire due to a ruptured oil line but the Belgian managed to put it out and continued losing nearly seven minutes.

In the second special Markko Märtin set the fastest time ahead of François Duval and after three specials the Ford drivers filled the first two places. Their speed was impressive and the Focus lived up to its promises of reliability. And their rivals? There were after all 80 entries. Up front Marcus Grönholm and Richard Burns drove as best they could but they were at a disadvantage by having to set off first, a really big handicap on the dry, dusty Greek roads. Rovanperä whose starting position was ideal, was not very quick but improved during the day to post 3 scratch times in 3 consecutive specials. Tommi Mäkinen shone briefly early on and was third for a time before being overtaken by Grönholm, who was again flat out in the specials second time round as the gravel was a lot cleaner evening things out. Markko Märtin controlled this first leg despite

McRae was one of the favourites before the start but he messed up his rally.

Solberg lost second place on the second day due to broken transmission.

a problem in the fifth special, Elatia-Zeli, when his Ford's bonnet suddenly blew up depriving him of visibility! Any other driver would have stopped to carry out repairs but not Markko. "I saw that there was a small circular arc between the bottom of the windscreen and the bonnet through which I could see the road," he explained later. "The problem was that I could not see beyond the end of the bonnet. I turned as soon as Michael Park (his co-driver) read off the notes without seeing the corner. We went off several times. It seemed to me a hell of a long time!" After twenty kilometres covered in this fashion he lost only six seconds to pacesetter Rovanperä!

Behind, the rest tried as best they could to catch the flying Estonian. McRae's engine took five minutes to fire up for the start of special no.2 and he received a 50 second penalty. Loix ran into more difficulties in special no.3 after his problems in the first leg while Burns was delayed by a spin in the same special and then

Sainz was again on the rostrum and took over second place in the championship.

Burns conserved his championship lead thanks to his fifth place and Grönholm's retirement.

Panizzi loves this kind of broken terrain. He drove fantastically well on Friday and Sunday but was not at his best on Saturday finally coming home seventh.

suffered gearbox problems in specials 4 and 5. Grönholm and Solberg both made driving errors in special no.4 and Pykälisto and Duval in specials nos 3 and 5 somersaulted off the road ending their rally on the spot. The world champion then retired after his car was afflicted by fuel pressure problems on the final liaison to Lamia only six kilometres from the service park. His results in the last six rallies read: three wins and three retirements two of which were down to his team because of his 206's lack of reliability. His exit took some of the pressure off Märtin even though Rovanperä's Peugeot was only 4.8 secs behind while Solberg in third was a further 23 seconds down.

Harri's threat was short-lived and in the Bauxites section on the second

day he suffered gearbox problems (the Achilles' Heel of the Peugeots in the Acropolis) leaving him with only 1st and 4th and the gap between himself and the Ford opened out to 1m 44s. Burns had already been handicapped the previous day because of the same problem and he met with even more trouble during the second leg as his 206 refused to select second. Knowing that it had been replaced the day before the Englishman had to put up with this handicap until the end of the rally. Which he did with considerable skill!

When Rovanperä slowed Solberg took over second but Märtin soon dispelled any illusions the young Norwegian might have entertained by setting four out of eight scratch times in the second leg. In addition, Petter lost

one minute due to broken transmission and came under threat from wily old Carlos Sainz who had made a cautious start to the event. His early tyre choice penalised him but as the rally wore on he upped the pace during the second leg and slipped past Solberg in mid-afternoon. The two fought a fantastic duel right up to the very end. The Subaru driver went flat out and despite setting seven scratch times he could not get past the Spaniard, and his task was not helped when he had to follow in the wake of Colin McRae, slowed by electronic gremlins, during the second-last special. He finally finished in a well-deserved third place while Sainz came home second. Richard Burns managed to bring his limping 206 to the flag in fourth taking advantage of the

Mäkinen has never won in Greece and his last appearance was no exception.

McRae was dominated by his team-mates.

Cyprus

Solberg was in top form and won a rally, which saw a large number of retirements caused by the gruelling nature of the layout. The Norwegian coolly controlled his speed and drove an intelligent race giving the new Subaru Impreza its first world championship victory.

THE RALLY
Oh Happy Man !

It was Petter Solberg's first win of the season.

Of course every rule has to have its exception and in Cyprus Petter Solberg was the odd man out. Why ? Because he openly admitted that he liked the event which almost qualifies as an extreme sports challenge ! There is the scorching heat, which in June-especially this year-can become unbearable, for example this year the ground temperature exceeded 50° and in the cars it varied between 60 and 65°. The stages are slow and twisty and give the cars no respite. Speedwise the longest stage (Lagoudera-Spilia, 38 kilometres) was covered at an average of 66,63 km/h, half that of Finland. Petter Solberg just detached himself completely from these problems. "Here you have to drive differently," he explained the day before the start. "As it's long and hot you have to know how to pace yourself and the car. You have to nurse it and look after the tyres and you mustn't be too hard on it with sudden bursts of acceleration. You have to really push and then lower the rhythm to give the Impreza some

Auriol set some quick times despite a sprained wrist but his car's reliability again let him down.

breathing space." His recipe for success was patience, caution and intelligence, pretty amazing for a driver known for his hot-headedness ! "I don't want to make any mistakes during the first leg, just to stay in contact with the quickest and then up the pace next day and really go flat out on Sunday if necessary. That's what I wanted to do in Greece but I had mechanical problems." He followed this strategy to the letter and on the last day he was not obliged to really push as his main rivals had all fallen by the wayside.

On Friday, Solberg adopted a smooth and cautious driving style leaving the fireworks up to Rovanperä. In contrast to his team-mates Harri was helped by his place in the starting order which was not the case for Burns and Grönholm. They were first and third in each special and they had to clear away the layer of little stones that covered the Cypriot mule trails the world champion doing a much better job than his team-mate. In addition to Rovanperä others took advantage of starting well back like Didier Auriol whose fantastic time left him in third place after the first stage. The rally was decided in the second passages through the four stages each of which had to be covered twice. It was here that Grönholm again showed his immense talent on clean routes and in

the final special of the day he blew everybody off with the exception of Loeb who conceded only 1.5 secondes despite a spin, and took the lead from the unfortunate Rovanperä. The latter was again the victim of gearbox problems like in Greece but still managed to hang onto second place and his hopes of victory. Solberg finished the day in third followed by the Panizzi brothers, Loeb and McRae.

The only significant retirement during the first leg was Justin Dale in the Hyundaï WRC even though several crews had problems due to the tough nature of the event. Loix and Schwartz were afflicted by engine overheating and differential problems and both Märtin and Burns's mounts suffered from falling hydraulic pressure. Duval's gearbox got stuck in fourth and then his brakes faded while Mäkinen kissed the rocks breaking his power steering.

But it was only the start ! In the second leg there was a raft of retirements. The new Focuses were the first to go in the opening stage of

Armin Schwarz was delayed by his engine overheating and differential problems.

Rovanperä drove a great rally until he was again delayed by mechanical problems.

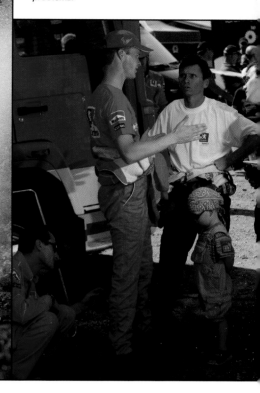

A chat between Panizzi and Rovanperä. In such conditions the Frenchman had little to envy the Finn.

Fréquelin watched the rally among the spectators on the side of the stages, as is his wont.

the day. Dust seeped into their engines and saturated the air filters. It then got mixed up in the oil and blocked the valve in the oil pump resulting in a big fall in pressure. It was all part of the learning curve for the young team that had done so well in the Acropolis but the Cypriot stages were that much tougher than the Greek ones. During the same special the transmission on Grönholm's 206 broke between the front and central differentials forcing the Finn to continue with only two-wheel drive. However, he was forced to retire in the next stage abandoning the lead to Solberg who had been much quicker in no.5 than Rovanperä. In the same special where Grönholm's rally ended (no.6 Asinou-Nikitari) more names joined the list of retirements including Loix and Panizzi with blown engines and Mäkinen again made involuntary contact with a rock breaking his Subaru's suspension and losing twenty-seven minutes. In no.9 Gardemeister crashed out of the event. Richard Burns was not destined to go much further as the championship leader's engine was showing signs of weakness in the same special. He managed to struggle through no.10 but gave up the ghost on the following liaison stage, which also proved fatal to Auriol's Skoda (electronics) as the heat had melted an alternator lead ! In no.11 Pykälisto's 206's engine went and

finally Tommi Mäkinen was given a reprieve in the second leg. Following his off in special no.6 he arrived at the start of the seventh stage over twenty minutes late enough to warrant exclusion. Which only became effective four stages further on. Thus the Finn was able to test his Impreza's reliability for his stable companion's benefit.

This spate of retirements robbed the rally of any suspense. Rovanperä tried to fight back but Solberg was always able to go one better. The Citroëns had all come through more or less intact with the exception of McRae, who had to stop on the road section coming back from special no.10 to repair the left-hand rear suspension mounting point, which he managed to do with the help of Derek Ringer his co-driver. At the end of the second leg Solberg came back to Limasol firmly installed in the lead from the last surviving Peugeot driver Rovanperä and the three Citroëns in the hands of Loeb, McRae and Sainz respectively. In the final leg nobody really pushed and Solberg set five scratch times out of the six possible. Peugeot ordered Rovanperä to bring the 206 home in second place enabling the team to add eight points to its total in the Manufacturers Championship. And it was no easy task because his transmission began to fail as the rally ended. Nonetheless the Finn managed

to fight off Sébastian Loeb on a final charge that took him to within 2.8 secondes of the red 206. Loeb was a happy man as it was his first rostrum finish on gravel. Behind the Alsatian came McRae and Sainz giving Citroën the highest accumulated number of points, eleven as against ten for Subaru and eight for Peugeot. It was not enough, however, to give the company with the chevron badge first place in the Manufacturers Championship. In the chase for the drivers title Burns left Cyprus still in the lead as his major rivals either

Panizzi was deprived of a good result when his engine blew during the second leg.

7

Hiroven's sixth place gave him his first world championship points. He respected his boss's advice to take care to the letter.

Grönholm led briefly, was slowed by broken transmission and then retired at the start of the second leg.

scored nothing (Grönholm and Märtin) or only 4 points in the case of Sainz. Solberg jumped several places up the hierarchy thanks to the ten points awarded for victory.

Subaru had another cause for celebration as in addition to Solberg's win the Japanese manufacturer also triumphed in Group N thanks to the efforts of Toshi Araï. It was his third consecutive success in four events counting towards the FIA Production Championship. He was the only one who really dared to push as in keeping with what happened to the Juniors in the Acropolis the main aim of the drivers was to finish. He came home first from the other Subarus of Rowe and Blomqvist thus increasing his lead in the championship. ∎

MID SEASON SUMMARY
Peugeot under pressure

With seven rounds gone the situation in the different championships was as follows : in the Drivers one Richard Burns had used the new points system to his advantage. He knew that in the same car-or indeed any other-he could never match Marcus Grönholm's pace so he settled for scoring the maximum number of points possible in each event like a penny pinching shopkeeper. What he did not realise was that if he were to win the title in this fashion he would be the laughing stock of motor sport.

Keke Rosberg has become famous for his incredible car control and to a lesser degree for being only the second driver to have won the F1 World Championship with one victory during the season (the other being Mike Hawthorn in 1958). In 2001, Burns did the same in rallying but without the same flamboyance. Would 2003 be a repeat performance but this time with zero wins ? Carlos Sainz, second as the teams tackled the second half of the season, had really gone for it. He won in Turkey, just missed out on another victory in Argentina and gave Petter Solberg one hell of a fight in the Acropolis setting scratch times despite the disadvantage represented by a new car and new co-driver. In addition, Burns had no right to use the excuse of being the first away on gravel as this is the role of the world championship leader. When Tommi Mäkinen was in his heyday he often had this task, never complained and scored some incredible victories. At the half-way mark Burns had set scratch times in 11 out of 131 specials and had never led a rally whereas Sainz had notched up 17 special stage wins and one outright victory. The Spaniard showed the same race intelligence as Burns scoring points five times out of seven compared to six for the Englishman. On the other hand Marcus Grönhom was the driver to have suffered the most under the new regulations : three wins-30 points-and four zeros even though the Finn had won 39

specials. He was still in line for the title but Peugeot had to overcome its reliability problems. The threat to Burns could also come from young chargers as the last two rallies had been won by Märtin and Solberg while Loeb had triumphed in Monte Carlo. What they still lacked was race craft but were much stronger on asphalt than Burns. The latter's skills resembled those of the cart horse while the former were thoroughbreds. The four rounds coming up on asphalt were enough to give the Englishman a few sleepless nights !

For Peugeot these events represented a way of restoring its credibility as while the 206 was still a remarkable weapon its reliability left a lot to be desired. Was this because it had been under pressure since the start of the season ? Whatever the case retaining the title looked like being an uphill struggle for the French manufacturer. And what was even more extraordinary was that its main threat came from Citroën, a part of the PSA Company ! The newcomer had made a big impression in its first full season by doing far better than expected with two wins by Loeb and Sainz in a car that was always among the front-runners. McRae on the other hand was victim of a certain amount of bad luck but seemed to have lost some of his fire. Luckily for the two French manufacturers Ford-and to a lesser extent Subaru with the 2003 Impreza- had taken some time to get its new Focus working properly as it

had become the benchmark in the WRC category. Hanging on to the crown would have been even more difficult if the Ford had made its debut in Monte Carlo. One thing that could be said, however, was that thanks to all the uncertainty generated since the start of the year rarely had a championship been so closely fought. So much the better ! ∎

Deutschland

Sébastian Loeb came out on top at the end of a gripping rally from Marcus Grönholm. Behind these two Märtin made a big impression in his new Ford Focus in the car's first test on asphalt demonstrating that it would be a force to be reckoned with in the future.

8

It was a repeat of 2002 with Marcus Grönholm finishing 2nd behind Sébastian Loeb to whom he was never a threat; an encouraging result for the Finn after two consecutive retirements.

Carlos Sainz, François Chatriot and Sébastian Loeb. It was the Citroën team's third win of the season, Loeb's second. Only Colin McRae had failed to open his score.

Mitsubishi was there to prepare for 2004. Its driver choice was a bit surprising as young Finns Jani Paasonen (here) and Kristian Sohlberg were not really asphalt specialists.

THE RACE
Loeb has the upper hand

At the time control at the start of the final stage, St Wendeler Land 2, Sebastian Loeb, in the lead from halfway through the second leg, appeared relaxed and confident. He was 13 seconds ahead of Marcus Grönholm with just over 18,93 km to go. Since the start of the rally there had been a fantastic battle that had resolved itself into a duel the day before between the Finn and the Alsatian. Grönholm went over to Loeb and said : "That's it. You're too quick on asphalt. I won't try and catch you." Everybody in the rally world knows what a nice guy Marcus is and he is

one of the most popular drivers in the championship. But he is also a past master of the art of the harmless little remark that can destabilise his adversaries. Ask Richard Burns ! Never again, though, will he fool Loeb. "I believed him," said the Frenchman later on. "I called Carlos who had finished the stage and he told me it was very tricky because of the mud. I wanted to ensure my first place so I didn't push from the start." It didn't make any real difference over the first section in relation to the Peugeot but at the end of the second where Guy Fréquelin himself was doing the timing, Sébastian was in for a nasty surprise. Grönholm had made up 10 seconds and there were only 10 kilometres to go ! During the first

eight the Peugeot had been over a second quicker per kilometre than the Xsara. At this rate Loeb would lose the rally. His team shouted the news to him in the Xsara's cockpit and he immediately understood that by trying to do just the minimum necessary following Grönholm's declaration of a non-aggression pact he was in grave danger of coming second. The conditions at the end of the stage were bad, much dirtier and slippier than the beginning. Sébastian let it all hang out taking unbelievable risks ! The flying Citroën reached the finish and its driver complained bitterly thinking that the Finn tricked him out of victory. The times were posted and he realised that his last minute sprint had succeeded as he was just

3.6 secondes ahead ! Sébastian and Daniel Elena had just won their third WRC Rally and the second on German territory not too far from the French border and a stone's throw from Loeb's natal Alsace.

The nail-biting finish crowned three days of hard driving. Right from the start of the rally the main contenders for victory threw themselves into the battle like sharks in a feeding frenzy led by Richard Burns. For once the world championship could really go flat out as he did not have to sweep away the dust, which was usually the case on gravel surfaces. He immediately set three consecutive scratch times putting him in the lead in a world championship rally for the

Markko Märtin was the only one able to keep up with Loeb. He had gearbox problems when in the lead and a penalty dropped him to fifth place. He was the star of the rally.

The photographers love Gilles Panizzi. However, the 'king of the asphalt' hadn't much to write home about in a rally that is not his cup of tea that ended in a lowly tenth place.

first time this season ahead of Grönholm who was also out to win his first rally on tarmac and the winner of the previous year's event Sébastien Loeb. Like his team-mates his task was not made any easier by the tyre choice. All the Citroëns were shod with Baumholder rubber (the name of the military camp used by the rally) which performed very inconsistently. The Frenchman did an excellent damage-limitation exercise but was forced to let the Peugeot and the Focus past. Up to then the Ford had shown its speed on gravel and the Estonian, who was no slouch on asphalt, demonstrated the car's enormous potential on tarmac. As Ford was now supplied by Michelin it had the best tyres for this surface like Peugeot and Citroën. The 2003 version of the Ford powered by a brilliant engine and helped by ideal weight distribution, a very low centre of gravity and aerodynamics worthy

of a car designed for circuit racing plus a sump that looked like a flat bottom set the road alight and Märtin found himself in the lead after setting the quickest times in SS 3 and 4. It was all too brief, however as in the fifth stage, Stein und Wein, the gearbox got its ratios all mixed up due to an hydraulic leak. Märtin was obliged to change gear manually and lost 50 seconds plus the lead. No longer in contention for victory he had nothing to lose (in contrast to the potential victors) and went pedal to metal setting several more scratch times much to the delight of the crowd. The fact that he was lucky with the weather often passing between showers did nothing to detract from his performance. He set 10 scratch times out of a possible 22 and finished the rally with the best performer award. "We'll be able to fight for victory in Corsica," said Christian Loriaux, the Ford chief

Just one point for Petter Solberg but one that would make the difference at the end of the season. It was his worst performance on tarmac this year.

Carlos Sainz's sixth place was the lowest of the three Citroëns at the finish. He beat François Duval's Ford by nine seconds.

engineer at the end of the rally. Good news for the PSA boys ! On the evening of the first leg Richard Burns came back to Trèves in the lead with 9.4 and 10.3 secondes in hand over Grönholm and Loeb. Colin McRae in fourth was already nearly 30 seconds behind. In fifth was Gilles Panizzi (43.1 secs back) who was never really in the hunt despite his tarmac skills because he had not raced in the event in 2002 and was suffering from a broken shoulder plus the sequels of an accident just before the rally in which he cracked a rib. Sainz was in sixth putting French cars in the first six places with François Duval breaking the tricolour hegemony ahead of Cedric Robert.

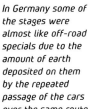

In Germany some of the stages were almost like off-road specials due to the amount of earth deposited on them by the repeated passage of the cars over the same route.

Philippe Bugalski's first rally of the year for Citroën in a car entered by the Spanish team Piedrafita ended with a blown engine.

Cédric Robert drove another good rally in the Bozian Team 206 WRC (as in Monte Carlo) finishing ahead of Gilles Panizzi but this time failed to score any points.

The second leg was much trickier than the first following nighttime showers which made the surface very slippery. Grönholm was on hand-cut slicks and set the quickest time on the first special. Then with Loeb on his tail, he snatched first place from Burns in the second stage. Märtin was in attack mode and set scratch times in several specials but it was of little consequence in the overall picture. He was in tenth place at the start of this leg which he finished in third. When it was time to tackle Panzerplatte-West, the eleventh stage the rain arrived

just to add spice to the proceedings. It was light when the first drivers went through and after Märtin passed it began to intensify causing all kinds of headaches for those on slicks. Burns dropped back in his usual anonymous fashion and made a couple of mistakes. Panizzi had to battle with his brakes. Solberg and Gardemeister broke their suspension and Paasonen had a big accident, luckily without injury that caused the interruption of the stage. Before this, though, McRae, Grönholm, Loeb and Duval had all set fantastic times in these difficult road

conditions. Panzerplatte second time round was less of a problem and an all-fired up Loeb nipped past Grönholm into the lead helped by a few minor driving errors on the part of the Finn who kept up the pressure on the Alsatian until the end of the leg. Before the teams returned to Tréves Roman Kresta (Peugeot 206 WRC) set his first ever scratch time in the world championship in the final stage, the St Wendel Super Special. There were still 6 stages to go on the Sunday. The gap between the two leaders was only 5.5 secondes In

Colin McRae failed to catch Richard Burns by ten seconds and rejoin his team-mate Loeb on the rostrum so Citroën pulled back only one point on Peugeot.

Reigning Junior Champion young Catalan Dani Sola was in his element on tarmac winning the Group N category in his Mitsubishi Lancer.

Carlos Sainz was the first foreigner to win the old "1000 Lakes Rally" in 1992. This time round he had be content with scoring a few precious points.

Märtin was in no mood to accept being passed by the Peugeot and he really piled on the pressure at the end of the stage, a little perturbed by storms, and got back in front of Grönholm who was still as incisive as ever. It was a piece of bravura driving on the part of the Estonian and at the end of the first ten stages he was 2.6 secs ahead of the Finn, 24.2 secs up on Burns. McRae and Solberg were already 50 secs behind.

There's nothing Grönholm loves more than a battle and he is never as strong as when he is under pressure. Stage no.12 was the tricky Ouninpohja special first time round over 33.24 kms and he put on a superb show snatching back the lead. "If Markko ups the pace again then I'll go even quicker," he promised. "Here you've got to surpass yourself," said Märtin. "That's what Marcus is doing." Just afterwards the Estonian thought that his chances had been destroyed as his Ford's electronics began to play up in stages 13 and 14. Its engine was not running correctly, the differentials went on the blink, the gear change went awry and the dashboard screen read out was defective. It seemed that his chances of fighting on equal terms had been blown. But help was at hand as the 206's lack of reliability again reared its head. In Ouninpohja second time round the right-hand front wheel of the Peugeot made a break for freedom after being compressed and it did not take Marcus' engineers long to find the reason: a broken wheel bearing. The damage had been done. The house of Peugeot was trembling on its very foundations as it was unable to give its star driver a car worthy of his talents; a major blunder when the manufacturers title is your prime objective.

Grönholm retirement did not really do much for Märtin's mood but luckily the Ford engineers managed to find and then cure the problems afflicting the Focus's engine management system. With his main rival hors de combat and Burns almost a day behind (1m 13s at the end of the second leg) the Estonian only had to keep it between the pine trees until the finish to score his second world championship victory. When he climbed onto the rostrum he faced a forest of black, white and blue flags waved by his fellow countrymen from nearby Estonia. This win put him back in the title chase at just the right moment.

Burn was the big loser in Finland and his decision to go for a points finish led to him being passed by Petter Solberg at the end of the rally as well as by an on-form Carlos Sainz slowed by a broken damper. The Spaniard's fourth place was the highest by a member of the Citroën squad. McRae had occupied the same place for a long time until he had a big accident during the second leg destroying a completely new car. He also received a

The world champion, however, did his very best right from the start to rack up his fourth consecutive win in his own country. Already in the Super Special organised on Thursday evening the day before the beginning of hostilities Markko Martin's win in his Ford FocusWRC03 gave a taste of what was to come. And he followed it up by setting the quickest times in four specials in which retirements and other incidents dashed a lot of hopes. Auriol had to stop with a painful shoulder, the sequel of an old injury that started acting up again. Rovanperä lost 20 minutes after damaging his suspension when he hit a rock while cutting a corner. Mäkinen and Solberg also hit stones the Finn breaking a rim. In the fifth stage, Lankamaa, Markko was obliged to cede first place to the 206. "We take a lot of risks," Märtin explained. "The locals know the roads by heart while we use notes." Another difficulty for foreigners is the limit placed on reconnaissance which is no problem for the Finns (it was not the case when Auriol and Sainz won) and this makes experience even more important thus the Estonian's performance all the more impressive. Solberg, a consistent fifth despite an off in stage no.2 followed by a broken roll bar plus the front stabiliser bar twisted in stage no.5, tried to play down the Ford driver's achievement. "The roads in Estonia are very like those in Finland. I am driving at 100% but I can't match Marcus and Markko." Familiarity with the layout, instinctive under standing of this type of route, symbiosis with the car were all explanations coming from drivers completely unable to keep up with the pair duelling for the lead. And there was a grain of truth in them all. Richard Burns summed it up as follows: "It's a two horse race." It was not so long ago that the 2001 world champion had dared to take the fight to Grönholm on his home turf. Perhaps this was an era when he opened a dictionary and by accident his eye fell on the word 'panache.' He hasn't opened it since!

McRae had his first big accident since joining Citroën. He was a bit worked up after being penalised 1 minute for arriving at a control too early.

penalty for clocking in too early due to a mistake by his co-driver Derek Ringer. Loeb finished fifth on a surface that he is still learning ahead of Mäkinen slowed by mechanical gremlins. Back racing in this event was the great Ari Vatanen. The European Member of Parliament was at the wheel of a 206 WRC and was as happy as a sand boy keeping up a stream of amusing quips throughout the three days. "In Ouninpohja I drove like my grandmother would have done. Then I saw my times and I said to myself that my grandma was one hell of a quick driver!" The fifty-one year old thoroughly enjoyed himself and set pretty respectable times. It was a big P.R success for Peugeot as the 1981 World Champion is still a very big star in his own country. It was some compensation for Corrado Provera and his men as among the four major

manufacturers entered in the world champion Peugeot was the one which scored the fewest points. Luckily for them Citroën only bagged three more but they brought Guy Fréquelin's team to within four points of the Sochaux firm's lead in the Manufacturers Championship.

JUNIORS
Tirabassi confirms

Finland was the fourth of the seven rallies on the 2003 Junior World Championship calendar. It was much more suited to the 2-wheel drive cars than the previous round, the Acropolis. Although Simon Jean-Joseph was not entered for this championship he had the same Clio as Tirabassi and was determined to score another win in the A6 category open

to the Super 1600s. He went off in the sixth stage and in the following one destroyed his Renault after taking off over a bump. The start of the rally was marked by a duel between the championship leader Brice Tirabassi and the Suzuki driver Daniel Carlsson. The Frenchman held onto the lead until he was victim of a puncture in stage no.13 followed by suspension problems that handed victory to Carlsson. He did not try to close the big gap between himself and the Swede and the latter gave the Suzuki Ignis its first world championship win to the great delight of Mr. Suzuki who was present at the finish. Yet another blow to Finnish pride! It was the halfway mark in the Junior Championship and the four rallies up to then had been won by three different manufacturers: Renault, Volkswagen and Suzuki. The

Since his 5 consecutive wins in this event earning him the title 'King of the Rally' Tommi Mäkinen has not really shone and this year he finished in a discrete 6th place.

domination of the Citroën Saxo seemed ages ago but its only rival was the Fiat Punto. The reigning French champion left Finland with 28 points 10 more than the winner of the event. He was followed like his shadow by Canellas from Spain (fifth in Finland) and the promising Estonian, Aava. After four events Tirabassi had proved that he was at home on all kinds of surfaces with top class performances in Monte Carlo, Greece and Finland. He was more than ever favourite for the title as two of the three remaining events on the calendar were on asphalt (Sanremo and Catalonia) with the final round in Great Britain. Marcos Liagato from Argentina had been one of the pre-season favourites but had never really been able to mix it with the front-runners as his Punto was a lot slower than the Ignis, the Clio and the Polo. Hopefully, this year's champion will not find himself in the same situation as Daniel Sola, the 2002 winner. After a brilliant season the Spaniard did not find a drive in the WRC (which is the aim of the competition) apart from a few furtive outings in a Xsara. ■

Once again Burns saved Peugeot's bacon. The same wheel-bearing problem as Grönholm deprived him of 2nd place but Corrado Provera was relieved.

Sebastian Lindholm, Marcus's brother-in-law and Peugeot Finland driver, came home 8th behind his young compatriot, Janne Tuohino in his private Ford Focus.

Sébastian Loeb learns quickly. He made no mistakes in what was his first real outing in the fastest rally of the year.

After Markku Alen in 2001, Ari Vatanen made a much-appreciated comeback in a 206. He spent most of the time waving to his many fans.

9th Leg of the 2003 World Rally Championship for constructors and drivers. **4th** leg of WRC Junior Championship.

Date: 6th to 10th August 2003

Route
1727,6 km divided in three legs
23 special stages on dirt roads
(411,19 km)

Superspecial
Thursday 7th August: (19h00):
Killeri (2,05 km)
1st leg
Friday 8th August (07h30-21h02):
Jyvaskyla > Pavilijonki > Jyvaskyla,
623,05 km; 9 special stages (142,43 km)
2nd leg
Saturday 9th August (06h30-19h48):
Jyvaskyla > Pavilijonki > Jyvaskyla,
745,52 km; 7 special stages (167,89 km)
3rd leg
Sunday 10th August (08h00-15h28):
Jyvaskyla > Pavilijonki > Jyvaskyla,
359,03 km; 6 special stages (100,87 km)

Entry List - Starters - Finishers
79 - 71 - 35

Conditions
changing weather, mainly dry roads, intermittent rain.

Results

WRC

	Driver/Navigator	Car	Gr.	Time
1	Märtin - Park	Ford Focus RS WRC 03	A	3h21'51"7
2	Solberg - Mills	Subaru Impreza WRC 2003		+58"9
3	Burns - Reid	Peugeot 206 WRC		+1'00"1
4	Sainz - Marti	Citroën Xsara WRC		+1'59"0
5	Loeb - Elena	Citroën Xsara WRC		+2'48"7
6	Mäkinen -Lindstrom	Subaru Impreza WRC 2003		+3'25"2
7	Tuohino - Aho	Ford Focus RS WRC 02		+4'22"9
8	Lindholm - Hantunen	Peugeut 206 WRC		+4'39"5
9	Pykälistö - Mertsalmi	Peugeot 206 WRC		+6'23"4
10	Loix - Smeets	Hyundai Accent WRC3		+8'19"9
11	Vatanen - Repo	Peugeot 206 WRC		+8'19"9
19	Carlsson - Andersson	Suzuki Ignis Super 1600	Jr.	+30'31"2

Leading Retirements (36)

ES19	Duval - Prevot	Ford Focus RS WRC 03	Accident
ES19	Välimäki - Honkanen	Hyundai Accent WRC³	Accident
ES16	C. McRae - Ringer	Citroën Xsara WRC	Accident
ES15	Grönholm - Rautiainen	Peugeut 206 WRC	Wheel bearing
ES13	Gardemeister - Lukander	Skoda Fabia WRC	Engine
ES12	Rovanperä - Pietiläinen	Peugeut 206 WRC	Accident
ES12	Hirvonen - Lehtinen	Ford Focus RS WRC 02	Fire
CH1B	Auriol - Giraudet	Skoda Fabia WRC	Injured shoulder

1 Marcus GRÖNHOLM - Timo RAUTIAINEN Peugeot 206 WRC

2 Richard BURNS - Robert REID Peugeot 206 WRC

3 Harri ROVANPERÄ - Risto PIETILÄINEN Peugeot 206 WRC

4 Markko MÄRTIN - Michael PARK Ford Focus RS WRC 03

5 Francois DUVAL - Stèphane PREVOT Ford Focus RS WRC 03

6 Mikko HIRVOVEN - Jarmo LEHTINEN Ford Focus RS WRC 02

7 Petter SOLBERG - Philip MILLS Subaru Impreza WRC 2003

8 Tommi MÄKINEN - Kaj LINDSTROM Subaru Impreza WRC 2003

10 Armin SCHWARZ - Manfred HIEMER Hyundai Accent WRC³

11 Freddy LOIX- Sven SMEETS Hyundai Accent WRC³

12 Jussi VÄLIMÄKI - Jakke HONKANEN Hyundai Accent WRC³

14 Didier AURIOL - Denis GIRAUDET Skoda Fabia WRC

15 Toni GARDEMEISTER - Paavo LUKANDER Skoda Fabia WRC

17 Colin McRAE- Derek RINGER Citroën Xsara WRC

18 Sébastien LOEB - Daniel ELENA Citroën Xsara WRC

19 Carlos SAINZ - Marc MARTI Citroën Xsara WRC

20 Jari-Matti LATVALA - Miikka ANTTILA Ford Focus RS WRC 02

21 Antony WARMBOLD - Gemma PRICE Ford Focus RS WRC 02

22 Juuso PYKÄLISTÖ - Esko MERTSALMI Peugeot 206 WRC

23 Janne TUOHINO - Jukka AHO Ford Focus RS WRC 02

24 Sebastian LINDHOLM - Timo HANTUNEN Peugeut 206 WRC

25 Kaj KUISTILA - Kari JOKINEN Ford Focus RS WRC02

26 Ari VATANEN - Juha REPO Peugeot 206 WRC

27 Jari VIITA - Riku ROUSKU Ford Focus RS WRC 01

33 Alistair GINLEY - Rory KENNEDY Ford Focus RS WRC 01

34 Tobias JOHANSSON - Benny LOKANDER Toyota Corolla WRC

35 Henning SOLBERG - Cato MENKERUD Mitsubishi Lancer Evo 6

52 Daniel CARLSSON - Mattias ANDERSSON Suzuki Ignis Super 1600

54 Kosti KATAJAMÄKI - Jani LAAKSONEN Volkswagen Polo

58 Marco LIGATO - Ruben GARCIA Fiat Punto S 1600

61 Brice TIRABASSI - Jacques-Julien RENUCCI Renault Clio 1.6 16V

67 Alessandro BROCCOLI - Simona GIRELLI Opel Corsa Super 1600

69 Salvador CANELLAS - Xavier AMIGO Suzuki Ignis Super 1600

70 Guy WILKS - Phil PUGH Ford Puma

71 Urmo AAVA - Kuldar SIKK Suzuki Ignis Super 1600

Special Stage Times

SS1 Killeri I (2,05 km)
1.Märtin 1'18"6; 2.Grönholm +0"4;
3.Solberg +0"6; 4.Duval +0"7;
5.Loeb +0"8; 6.Burns/Rovanperä +0"9;
8.C. McRae +1"1...
Jr. (33) Carlsson +8"7

SS2 Jukojarvi I (22,30 km)
1.Grönholm/Märtin 10'50"8;
3.Solberg +5"9; 4.Burns +8"2;
5.C. McRae +10"3; 6.Pykälistö +10"4;
7.Tuohino +11"4; 8.Lindholm +11"5...
Jr. (31) Teuronen +1'21"9

SS3 Kruunupera I (22,30 km)
1.Märtin 9'12"4; 2.Grönholm +3"7;
3.C. McRae +7"4; 4.Burns +10"2;
5.Solberg/Sainz +12"0; 7.Mäkinen +13"9;
8.Tuohino +14"8...
Jr. (35) Carlsson +1'14"5

SS4 Valkola (8,42 km)
1.Grönholm 4'25"4; 2.Burns +0"7;
3.C. McRae +2"5; 4.Märtin +3"1;
5.Sainz +3"4; 6.Rovanperä/Solberg +3"5;
8.Tuohino +6"0...
Jr. (33) Wilks +43"4

SS5 Lankamaa (23,46 km)
1.Grönholm 11'26"0; 2.Burns +0"7;
3.Märtin +3"7; 4.Sainz +8"0;
5.Solberg +10"1; 6.Rovanperä +10"6;
7.C. McRae +10"7; 8.Loeb +12"5...
Jr. (35) Carlsson +1'44"5

SS6 Laukaa (11,81 km)
1.Märtin 5'46"1; 2.Grönholm +2"0;
3.Burns +4"7; 4.C. McRae +7"0;
5.Sainz +7"1; 6.Hirvonen +9"6;
7.Solberg +10"1; 8.Rovanperä +10"6...
Jr. (31) Teuronen +54"5

SS7 St. Ruu himaki (7,57 km)
1.Burns 4'03"4; 2.Grönholm +2"8;
3.Märtin +4"7; 4.Sainz +5"1;
5.Solberg +5"8; 6.Loeb +7"5;
7.C. McRae +8"2; 8.Hirvonen +9"1...
Jr. (32) Carlsson +38"3

SS8 Jukojarvi II (22,30 km)
1.Märtin 10'40"1; 2.Grönholm/Burns +1"6;
4.Solberg +4"7; 5.Sainz +6"5;
6.C. McRae +7"4; 7.Loeb +12"9;
8.Gardemeister +18"8...
Jr. (32) Tirabassi +1'51"7

SS9 Kruunupera II (20,17 km)
1.Märtin 9'03"0; 2.Grönholm +3"5;
3.C. McRae +5"6; 4.Loeb +6"3;
5.Burns +8"2; 6.Solberg +8"8;
7.Sainz +8"9; 8.Rovanperä 15"3...
Jr. (29) Carlsson +1'27"3

SS10 Killeri II (2,05 km)
1.Grönholm 1'19"1; 2.Märtin +0"1;
3.Solberg +0"3; 4.Burns/Rovanperä +0"6;
6.C. McRae +0"7; 7.Duval +0"8;
8.Loeb +0"8...
Jr. (34) Carlsson +11"0

SS11 Paijala (21,95 km)
1.Grönholm 11'21"4; 2.Märtin +1"9;
3.Rovanperä +2"8; 4.Burns +5"1;
5.C. McRae +5"4; 6.Solberg +10"1;
7.Sainz 11"5; 8.Loeb +13"8...
Jr. (30) Wilks +1'34"2

SS12 Ouninpohja I (33,24 km)
1.Grönholm 15'31"0; 2.Märtin +4"4;
3.C. McRae +8"8; 4.Burns +10"8;
5.Sainz +14"9; 6.Solberg +16"1;
7.Pykälistö +20"3; 8.Mäkinen 25"1...
Jr. (26) Carlsson +2'08"2

SS13 Urria (10,00 km)
1.Burns 4'48"4; 2.Grönholm/
C. McRae +2"1; 4.Sainz +2"3;
5.Solberg +2"9; 6.Märtin +3"0;
7.Mäkinen +3"6; 8.Loeb +4"1...
Jr. (28) Carlsson +36"9

SS14 Ouninpohja II (33,24 km)
1.C. McRae 15'25"1; 2.Burns +6"4;
3.Loeb +6"9; 4.Sainz +12"7;
5.Märtin +17"8; 6.Solberg +18"2;
7.Mäkinen +22"1; 8.Lindholm +23"7...
Jr. (27) Carlsson +2'05"5

SS15 Ehikki (14,90 km)
1.Burns 6'52"6; 2.Sainz +1"8;
3.C. McRae +2"8; 4.Märtin +6"3;
5.Lindholm +6"4; 6.Solberg +8"7;
7.Loeb +9"9; 8.Mäkinen 10"6...
Jr. (24) Carlsson +57"0

SS16 Moksi-Leustu (40,95 km)
1.Märtin 20'39"2; 2.Solberg +2"0;
3.Burns +3"7; 4.Sainz +4"3;
5.Loeb +8"8; 6.Märtin +10"2;
7.Lindholm +20"4; 8.Tuohino +22"6...
Jr. (23) Carlsson +3'14"3

SS17 Himos (13,61 km)
1.Solberg 7'30"1; 2.Märtin +1"3;
3.Sainz +3"8; 4.Mäkinen +5"4;
5.Loeb +5"5; 6.Lindholm +6"8;
7.Tuohino +9"0; 8.Loix +17"8...
Jr. (23) Carlsson +1'05"1

SS18 Parkkola I (19,87 km)
1.Märtin 9'53"0; 2.Solberg +1"3;
3.Burns +2"5; 4.Sainz +3"5;
5.Mäkinen +5"4; 6.Loeb +5"5;
7.Lindholm +10"7; 8.Tuohino 13"0...
Jr. (24) Wilks +1'21"1

SS19 Mokkipera I (13,96 km)
1.Burns 6'56"0; 2.Solberg +0"3;
3.Märtin +0"5; 4.Loeb +5"9;
5.Sainz +7"6; 6.Tuohino +7"7;
7.Pykälistö +8"1; 8.Lindholm +8"7...
Jr. (23) Carlsson +1'01"0

SS20 Palsankyla (25,45 km)
1.Burns 13'31"2; 2.Solberg +2"2;
3.Märtin +11"3; 4.Tuohino +17"7;
5.Pykälistö/Lindholm +20"6;
7.Loeb +22"7; 8.Sainz +23"1...
Jr. (19) Tirabassi +2'11"3

SS21 Kuohu (7,76 km)
1.Burns 3'45"3; 2.Märtin +1"1;
3.Solberg +1"3; 4.Sainz +4"9;
5.Mäkinen +5"0; 6.Lindholm +5"4;
7Pykälistö +9"6; 8.Tuohino +9"9...
Jr. (21) Svedlund +31"4

SS22 St. Parkkola II (19,87 km)
1.Solberg 9'39"7; 2.Burns +1"3;
3.Märtin +2"2; 4.Loeb +10"7;
5.Sainz +11"2; 6.Mäkinen +11"8;
7.Tuohino +18"7; 8.Lindholm +19"8...
Jr. (21) Carlsson +1'27"4

SS23 St. Mokkipera II (13,96 km)
1.Solberg 6'47"8; 2.Burns +3"0;
3.Märtin +4"6; 4.Pykälistö +8"5;
5.Tuohino +10"6; 6.Loeb +10"7;
7.Mäkinen +11"9; 8.Sainz +15"1...
Jr. (20) Carlsson +1'03"4

Championship Classifications

FIA Drivers (9/14)
1.Burns 49; 2.Sainz 44; 3.Grönholm 38; 4.Solberg 38; 5.Loeb 37; 6.Märtin 37;
7.C. McRae 28; 8.Mäkinen 18; 9.Rovanperä 16; 10.Duval 11; 11.Gardemeister 9;
12.Panizzi 6; 13.Auriol 4; 14.Hirvonen 3; 15.A. McRae 3; 16.Robert 3;
17.Schwarz 3; 18.Tuohino 2; 19.Ginley 1; 20.Lindholm 1

FIA Constructors (9/14)
1.Peugeot 101; 2.Citroën 97; 3.Ford 60; 4.Subaru 60; 5.Skoda 20; 6.Hyundai 10

FIA Junior WRC (4/7)
1.Tirabassi 28; 2.Carlsson 18; 3.Canellas 17; 4.Aava 16; 5.Wilks 15;
6.Katajamäki 10; 7.Ligato 10; 8.Broccoli 9; 9.Svedlund 5; 10.Teuronen 5;
11.Ceccato 4; 12.Cecchettini 4; 13.Feghali 3; 14.Sebalj 3; 15.Baldacci 2; 16.Iliev 2;
17.Harrach 1

FIA Production Car WRC (5/7)
1.Arai 30; 2.Rowe 27; 3.Singh 22; 4.Blomqvist 21; 5.Sola 18; 6.Ligato 13;
7.Al Wahaibi 6; 8.Kulig 6; 9.Trivino 6; 10.Bourne 5; 11.Errani 5; 12.Manfrinato 5;
13.Colsoul 4; 14.De Dominicis 4; 15.Ferreyros 4; 16.Holowczyc 4; 17.Roman 3;
18.Aur 2; 19.McShea 2; 20.Sztuka 2; 21.Marrini 1; 22.Richard 1

Performers

	1	2	3	4	5	6
Märtin	8	5	6	2	1	1
Grönholm	6	7	-	-	-	-
Burns	6	6	3	5	1	1
Solberg	3	4	1	4	1	6
C. McRae	1	1	5	1	2	2
Sainz	-	1	1	7	7	-
Loeb	-	-	1	3	3	3
Rovanperä	-	-	1	1	-	3
Mäkinen	-	-	-	1	2	2
Pykälistö	-	-	-	1	1	1
Tuohino	-	-	-	1	1	1
Duval	-	-	-	1	-	-
Lindholm	-	-	-	-	2	2
Hirvonen	-	-	-	-	-	1

Event Leaders

SS1 > SS4	Märtin
SS5 > SS8	Grönholm
SS9 > SS11	Märtin
SS12 > SS13	Grönholm
SS14 > SS23	Märtin

Previous winners

1973	Mäkinen - Liddon Ford Escort RS 1600	1988	Alen - Kivimaki Lancia Delta Integrale
1974	Mikkola - Davenport Ford Escort RS 1600	1989	Ericsson - Billstam Mitsubishi Galant VR4
1975	Mikkola - Aho Toyota Corolla	1990	Sainz - Moya Toyota Celica GT-Four
1976	Alen - Kivimaki Fiat 131 Abarth	1991	Kankkunen - Piironen Lancia Delta Integrale 16v
1977	Hamalaiinen - Tiukkanen Ford Escort RS	1992	Auriol - Occelli Lancia Delta Integrale
1978	Alen - Kivimaki Fiat 131 Abarth	1993	Kankkunen - Giraudet Toyota Celica Turbo 4WD
1979	Alen - Kivimaki Fiat 131 Abarth	1994	Mäkinen - Harjanne Ford Escort RS Cosworth
1980	Alen - Kivimaki Fiat 131 Abarth	1995	Mäkinen - Harjanne Mitsubishi Lancer Ev.3
1981	Vatanen - Richards Ford Escort RS	1996	Mäkinen - Harjanne Mitsubishi Lancer Ev.3
1982	Mikkola - Hertz Audi Quattro	1997	Mäkinen - Harjanne Mitsubishi Lancer Ev.4
1983	Mikkola - Hertz Audi Quattro	1998	Mäkinen - Mannisenmäki Mitsubishi Lancer Ev.5
1984	Vatanen - Harryman Peugeot 205 T16	1999	Kankkunen - Repo Subaru Impreza WRC
1985	Salonen - Harjanne Peugeot 205 T16	2000	Grönholm - Rautiainen Peugeot 206 WRC
1986	Salonen - Harjanne Peugeot 205 T16	2001	Grönholm - Rautiainen Peugeot 206 WRC
1987	Alen - Kivimaki Lancia Delta HF Turbo	2002	Grönholm - Rautiainen Peugeot 206 WRC

Daniel Carlsson

Australia

Australia

Once Marcus Grönholm had been eliminated due to a driving error the rally turned into a fantastic duel between Sébastian Loeb and Petter Solberg. The Frenchman led for most of the event before giving way to the Norwegian near the end and his fighting drive will be remembered for a long time.

THE RALLY
A spellbinding duel

The sixteenth Australian Rally was the type of thrilling event that happens once in a blue moon. Thanks to the skill and daring of the drivers, who were like tightrope artists working without a safety net, the spectators remained spellbound throughout. Marcus Grönholm loves down under and he has won the last three rallies on Australian soil. He was out to continue the series and also to see the flag following two consecutive retirements in the last two rallies. Apart from the first stage, a super special beloved of the Australians, which gave Solberg an early lead, the second in the countryside saw Grönholm hit the front after getting past Petter Solberg and Markko Märtin who were expected to shine in Australia having won the last two gravel events. Thanks to mistakes on the part of his rivals including those in a car park committed in Murray South by Loeb and Märtin, Richard Burns managed to get into the top three. True he was the first away which was a big disadvantage but half way through the first leg he was passed into third place by Sebastian Loeb, who was not expected to be really at home on this type of surface. It was a brilliant performance on the part of the Citroën driver given his unfamiliarity with the terrain. In fact his only outing in Australia was in 2002 after which he admitted feeling a bit at sea on this surface. It is an event that tames even the most skilful

as it combines a surface that resembles a coating of marbles with narrow tracks covered at high speeds in precarious conditions amid eucalyptus trees. A year later the fact that he was so well placed proved not only his talent but also the fact that his team had absorbed the lessons learnt during its first outing on Australian soil. The Citroën had made a lot of progress in the areas of driveability, suspension and differentials.

Grönholm dominated the event until Murray North second time round. It was the eighth stage on the programme and included a very tight uphill hairpin with a deep ditch on the inside of the track. First time round the Peugeot driver had gone very deeply into the corner using the torque to get round thanks to a violent burst of acceleration in first gear. He tried to do the same second time but got it all wrong and the 206 immediately tipped over. The marshals hesitated a little before allowing the few spectators present to intervene and they took a long time to put the car back on its wheels. This incident cost Grönholm nineteen minutes. Driver and co-driver were deeply disappointed and brought their car back to the service park where, with the agreement of their team, they withdrew, as they had no chance of finishing among the first eight point scorers. The world champion's stupid error cost him dear as it was his fourth retirement in five events and severely compromised his chances of retaining his title.

The Langley park super special has long been considered a yardstick and is still a fantastic spectacle despite changing sites.

Both Tommi Mäkinen and Markko Märtin messed up their rally. It was more problematic for the young Estonian than for the Finn as he compromised his title chances.

François Duval left with better memories than in 2002. If his performance did not grab the headlines at least he did not finish against a tree.

In Australia Sébastian Loeb drove his most convincing rally of the year. With three asphalt rallies to come he assumed the mantle of favourite for the drivers' title.

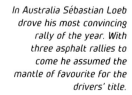

And who was now in the lead? None other but Sébastian Loeb in second place behind Marcus until the latter's misadventure. The Frenchman was in maximum attack mode and behind him Solberg gave as good as he got. Only François Duval managed to beat them both in the final stage of the leg, the same Mickey Mouse section as the day before. So Grönholm was out and the battle for supremacy was being fought out by two of rally's coming men Loeb and Solberg separated by only 4.1 secs. In third Burns was already 40 secs behind and the rest led by Mäkinen were a minute in arrears. The second leg turned into a nail-biting, hard-fought duel as each one sought to press home his advantage. Solberg set the first two scratch times but Loeb fought back to maintain his lead even though after the first day the time sheets showed the two drivers dead-heating for first place in the overall classification. There were 10 specials and both the Frenchman and the Norwegian took four each with Markko Märtin being quickest in the other two. The gaps were tiny as proved by the 5/10 of a second separating them at the end of the 17,31 Helena South stage.

In Australia Sébastian Loeb drove his most convincing rally of the year. With three asphalt rallies to come he assumed the mantle of favourite for the drivers' title.

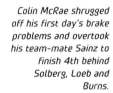

Colin McRae shrugged off his first day's brake problems and overtook his team-mate Sainz to finish 4th behind Solberg, Loeb and Burns.

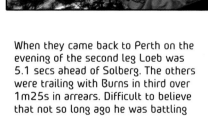

Solberg tried a bit of psychological warfare saying to anyone with ears to hear that a rally was not won on the Saturday but on Sunday so patience was of a premium. Loeb hit back by stating: "I'm completely confident. What I've gained today I don't have to pull back tomorrow." Solberg: "being second doesn't worry me. I prefer being the hunter rather than the hunted. I'm not on the limit. I've still got something in reserve." Loeb: "the tension doesn't let up." Each driver sought to undermine the other's confidence either on the routes or off them well aware that the media would repeat each dig. They were amazingly relaxed and professional as well as being courteous and respectful towards each other.

When they came back to Perth on the evening of the second leg Loeb was 5.1 secs ahead of Solberg. The others were trailing with Burns in third over 1m25s in arrears. Difficult to believe that not so long ago he was battling

Dani Solà worked hard for his 5th place in Group N (production cars) in his Mitsubishi Lancer on his first outing on Australian soil.

for victory in this event with McRae, Mäkinen, Sainz and Auriol who were miles behind. They all had their excuses. Mäkinen ran into gearbox problems followed by an off, Sainz went straight on, Auriol's machine's road holding was extremely erratic and both Burns and McRae's cars landed on their noses. Nothing too serious in fact except that Auriol was in a Skoda! Märtin was eliminated during the night. At the end of stage 18 a large stone fell out of his boot under the eyes of the marshals. What was it doing there? Illegal ballast (even though the Ford had tipped the scales at 1253 kilos, 23 over the limit) or a wedge for the spare as Ford claimed. Fnally the FIA excluded the Focus without really getting to the bottom of the story, which might have been just a clumsy precaution on the part of the team before going onto the scales. It cost the Estonian fourth place.

The final leg made up of the famous Bannister stages was in keeping with the tradition of the Australian event. Four sections measuring 117,11 kms remained to determine the outcome of the rally. For the first Loeb fitted the wrong tyres which were perfect for

Petter Solberg sportingly acknowledged that Loeb had been a constant threat. His win put him in 2nd place in the championship 7 points behind Burns.

Markko Märtin used a stone to replace the strap holding the spare wheel in place in his Focus. He was disqualified, as ballast must be securely fixed to the car floor.

Richard Burns limited the damage with another rostrum finish in his 206 WRC but this did not prevent Citroën from catching Peugeot in the Manufacturers' Championship.

the second. This error let Solberg into the lead but he retook the Norwegian in the next special helped by a sideways moment on the part of his adversary. A gap of 1.9 secs and 58 kilometres to go. Then the weather took a hand. Loeb set off on hard tyres

hoping for a dry surface while Solberg chose soft rubber. A heavy shower fell and that decided the result. Informed by a mini-message Loeb realised that the game was up, slowed knowing that he had lost too much time and settled for an excellent second place. Thus,

Solberg scored his third world championship victory, his second of the season, the same number as the Frenchman. "That guy forced me to take unbelievable risks," said Petter after the event paying homage to the pugnacity of his rival. This epic battle

put both drivers back in contention for the drivers' title. Burns was still in the lead but he was only 7 points ahead of the day's winner dead-heating with Sainz (fifth in Australia) and 10 in front of Loeb. Backed up by McRae (fourth) Citroën was now on level

Freddy Loix's 8th place gave Hyundaï two points in the championship. They were the last as the small Korean team withdrew from the championship after this event.

Harri Rovanperä's 7th position was a big comedown after his 2nd place last year.

By now Petter Solberg completely dominated his team-mate Tommi Mäkinen. The Finn came home 6th over 3 minutes behind the Norwegian in his last Australian rally.

pegging with Peugeot in the Manufacturers' Championship. With four rounds to go before the end of the season one could not have dreamed of a better scenario. In the Production Championship, the British driver Rowe won and went into the lead from the Japanese Araï and Singh from Malaysia. The driver of the white Subaru now had a 7-point lead and looked odds on to win the championship as there was only one event left on the Group N Calendar, the Tour of Corsica.

CONCLUSION
Young guns take over?

Märtin won in Greece and then Finland, Solberg in Cyprus and Australia and Loeb triumphed in Germany while just missing out on his first victory on gravel in Australia. The last five rallies had fallen to one of the three coming men. The only one who seemed able to do battle with them on equal terms was Marcus Grönholm but he had been let down too many times by his Peugeot 206's

Toni Gardemeister did not have an easy rally due to an arm injury especially when he had to inverse the wheels following a puncture.

poor reliability plus a few personal errors that prevented him from scoring probable victories. He had had a bad summer. The 2003 Drivers Championship title appeared to be slipping from his grasp and he admitted as much. But what about the others like Sainz, Mäkinen, Burns McRae and Auriol who had been the usual championship contenders over the past several seasons? The answer in the Frenchman's case was simple: Skoda. For the others the explanation was a bit more complicated. Burns and Sainz had both understood that the new points system demanded a different

approach. In Australia the Brit scored another third place his seventh rostrum finish out of 10 since Monte Carlo. Certainly his consistency had been a great help to Peugeot in the latter's chase of the Manufacturers title but by favouring consistency over speed he had compromised his own chances. Sainz showed more flair. He won in Turkey and could have done so again in Argentina. McRae fluctuated between good and bad but a bit like Grönholm at Peugeot he seemed to attract misfortune in the Citroën camp. And Mäkinen? The 4-times world champion was but a pale

shadow of his former self. Before the start of the Australian rally he announced his retirement at the end of the year, which, funnily enough, seemed to give him fresh motivation during the event. The main lesson to be drawn from a summer that had been dominated by the young guns was: would 2003 see a traditional champion like Sainz or Burns being crowned? Because if the answer was yes it would certainly be the last time as the new generation was poised to take over. ■

Ten points separated Sébastian Loeb and Richard Burns and he was now only 3 behind the Solberg/Sainz duo. Citroën and Peugeot were neck and neck. Was a double on the cards?

Even if his fan club had not come to Australia (distance!) Petter Solberg now has admirers everywhere.

10th Leg of the 2003 World Rally Championship for constructors and drivers. **6th** leg of FIA Production Car WRC Championship.

Date: 3rd to 7th September 2003

Route
1795,16 km divided in three legs
24 special stages on dirt road (386,22 km)

Superspecial
Thursday 4th September: (18h38)
Gloucester Park (2,45 km)
1st leg
Friday 5th September (06h00-20h40):
Perth > Jarrahdale > Perth 805,42 km;
10 special stages (145,17 km);
2nd leg
Saturday 6th September (07h30-19h58):
Perth > Jarrahdale > Perth, 515,13 km;
10 special stages (123,96 km)
3rd leg
Sunday 7th September (07h00-16h30):
Perth > Jarrahdale > Perth, 474,61 km;
4 special stages (117,09 km)

Entry List - Starters - Finishers
56 - 50 - 32

Conditions
rain, drying roads, showers on Sunday .

Results WRC

	Driver/Navigator	Car	Gr.	Time
1	**Solberg - Mills**	**Subaru Impreza WRC 2003**	**A**	**3h32'07"1**
2	Loeb - Elena	Citroën Xsara WRC		+26"6
3	Burns - Reid	Peugeot 206 WRC		+1'53"0
4	C. McRae - Ringer	Citroën Xsara WRC		+2'30"7
5	Sainz - Marti	Citroën Xsara WRC		+2'37"2
6	Mäkinen - Lindstrom	Subaru Impreza WRC 2003		+3'01"5
7	Rovanperä - Pietiläinen	Peugeot 206 WRC		+4'03"9
8	Loix - Smeets	Hyundai Accent WRC³		+7'00"7
9	Hirvonen - Lehtinen	Ford Focus RS WRC 03		+7'10"6
10	Duval - Prevot	Ford Focus RS WRC 03		+7'46"2
15	**Rowe - Agnew**	**Subaru Impreza WRX**	**Prod.**	**+22'10"0**

Leading Retirements (35)

CH20B	Märtin - Park	Ford Focus RS WRC 03	Excluded
ES14	Arai - Sircombe	Subaru Impreza WRX	Mechanical prob.
CH10D	Ligato - Garcia	Mitsubishi Lancer Evo 7	Mechanical prob.
CH9B	Grönholm - Rautiainen	Peugeut 206 WRC	Decided after accident
ES7	Jean-Joseph - Boyere	Mitsubishi Lancer Evo 6	Suspension
ES4	Ferreyros - Martin	Mitsubishi Lancer Evo 6	Mechanical prob.

Martin Rowe

Special Stage Times

SS1 Perth City Super I (2,45 km)
1.Solberg 1'31"9; 2.Sainz +0"3; 3.Märtin +0"7;
4.Mäkinen +0"9; 5.Burns/Rovanperä/
C. McRae/Loeb +1"1... FIA Prod. (18) Ligato +8"0

SS2 Murry North I (18,48 km)
1.Grönholm 10'29"1; 2. Solberg +2"4;
3.Märtin +6"4; 4.Loeb +7"2; 5.Mäkinen +12"3;
6.Burns +13"1; 7.Sainz +18"1; 8.C McRae +18"3...
FIA Prod. (16) Ligato +56"7

SS3 Murray South I (20,12 km)
1.Grönholm 11'51"8; 2.Sainz +9"1;
3.Solberg +9"7; 4.Burns +10"2; 5.Mäkinen +15"8;
6.Loeb +18"1; 7.Rovanperä +19"8;
8.C McRae 23"4... FIA Prod. (16) Ligato +1'05"9

SS4 Gobbys (5,19 km)
1.Märtin 2'29"6; 2.Solberg +1"6;
3.Hirvonen +1"8; 4.Loeb +1"9;5.Grönholm +2"1;
6.Mäkinen +2"8;7.Sainz +3"0; 8.Burns +4"3...
FIA Prod. (15) Ligato +15"6

SS5 Stirling West (15,89 km)
1.Loeb 9'15"3; 2.Solberg +0"5; 3.Grönholm +2"2;
4.Burns +5"3; 5.Märtin +7"5; 6.Rovanperä +8"7;
7.C McRae +9"6; 8.Mäkinen +10"3...
FIA Prod. (19) Ligato +50"7

SS6 Stirling Long (34,99 km)
1.Loeb 20'02"1; 2.Grönholm +8"0;
3.Burns +17"6; 4.Solberg +18"7;
5.Rovanperä +20"9; 6.Mäkinen +22"9;
7.Sainz +24"3; 8.C McRae +30"6...
FIA Prod. (18) Rowe +1'52"5

SS7 Turner Hill (7,00 km)
1.Solberg 4'22"4; 2.Grönholm +2"2;
3.Burns +3"0; 4.Loeb +3"5; 5.Sainz +4"5;
6.Mäkinen/C. McRae +6"1; 8.Rovanperä +9"4...
FIA Prod. (17) Singh +29"3

SS8 Murray North II (18,48 km)
1.Solberg/Loeb 10'14"4; 3.Märtin +0"9;
4.Mäkinen +5"2; 5.Burns +5"4; 6.C. McRae +8"3;
7.Loix +15"7; 8.Hirvonen +21"8...
FIA Prod. (16) N. McShea +58"3

SS9 Murray South II (20,12 km)
1.Loeb 11'30"0; 2.Solberg +3"1; 3.Märtin +5"7;
4.Grönholm +8"9; 5.Sainz +9"8; 6.Burns +10"4;
7.C McRae +14"1; 8.Mäkinen +16"0...
FIA Prod. (18) Arai +1'22"0

SS10 Perth City II (2,45 km)
1.Duval 1'33"5; 2.Märtin/Mäkinen +0"2;
4.Solberg/C. McRae +0"4; 6.Loeb +0"5;
7.Sainz +0"7; 8.Burns +1"0...
FIA Prod. (18) Blomqvist +7"2

SS11 Beraking East (8,88 km)
1.Solberg 5'09"6; 2.Loeb +1"2; 3.Burns +3"9;
4.Rovanperä +5"8 5.Mäkinen +7"3;
6.C. McRae +7"4; 7.Märtin +7"7; 8.Sainz +8"4...
FIA Prod. (17) Arai +30"5

SS12 Helena East I (20,48 km)
1.Solberg 11'38"2; 2.Loeb +2"7; 3.Burns +7"3;
4.Märtin +10"6; 5.Rovanperä +11"4;
6.C. McRae +12"1; 7.Sainz +12"7;
8.Mäkinen +13"9... FIA Prod. (17) Rowe +1'05"2

SS13 Helena West I (12,60 km)
1.Loeb 7'18"4; 2.Solberg +2"6; 3.C. McRae +5"7;
4.Burns +6"5; 5.Mäkinen +7"1; 6.Sainz +8"7;
7.Rovanperä +9"1; 8.Märtin 10"8...
FIA Prod. (16) Arai +42"1

SS14 Helena South II (17,30 km)
1.Solberg 8'55"3; 2.Loeb +0"4; 3.Burns +4"7;
4.Märtin +5"0; 5.C. McRae +5"1; 6.Mäkinen +6"9;
7.Sainz +8"6; 8.Rovanperä +9"2...
FIA Prod. (18) Rowe +57"3

SS15 Beraking West (9,42 km)
1.Solberg 4'38"7; 2.Loeb +1"2; 3.Märtin +3"5;
4.Burns +3"8; 5.Sainz +6"6; 6.Mäkinen +7"4;
7.C. McRae +8"9; 8.Rovanperä +9"5...
FIA Prod. (14) Sola +26"4

SS16 Helena East II (20,48 km)
1.Loeb 11'23"8; 2.Solberg +1"6; 3.Märtin +6"9;
4.Rovanperä +7"5; 5.Burns +8"9;
6.C. McRae +10"0; 7.Mäkinen +16"7;
8.Sainz +21"1... FIA Prod. (17) Sola +1'07"1

SS17 Helena West II (12,60 km)
1.Loeb 7'10"6; 2.Solberg +0"3; 3.Märtin +6"3;
4.Rovanperä +6"6; 5.Sainz +8"7; 6.C. McRae +8"7;
7.Burns +9"7; 8.Mäkinen +14"4...
FIA Prod. (17) Sola +42"6

SS18 Helena South II (17,30 km)
1.Loeb 8'46"6; 2.Solberg +2"4; 3.C. McRae +2"7;
4.Märtin +4"7; 5.Rovanperä +5"2; 6.Sainz +5"6;
7.Burns +6"2; Mäkinen +12"4...
FIA Prod. (17) Sola +53"9

SS19 Perth City Super III (2,45 km)
1.Märtin 1'31"7; 2.Mäkinen +0"7; 3.Solberg +0"8;
4.Loeb +1"0; 5.C. McRae +1"5; 6.Burns +1"7;
7.Sainz +1"8; 8.Duval +2"0...
FIA Prod. (16) Blomqvist +7"4

SS20 Perth City Super IV (2,45 km)
1.Märtin 1'31"8; 2.C. McRae +0"5;
3.Solberg +0"8; 4.Loeb/Sainz +1"0;
6.Mäkinen +1"3; 7.Burns/Duval +1"5...
FIA Prod. (14) Blomqvist +6"9

SS21 Bannister North (24,80 km)
1.Solberg 13'11"9; 2.Loeb +5"7; 3.Sainz +6"6;
4.Burns +9"4; 5.C. McRae +11"0;
6.Rovanperä +13"8; 7.Mäkinen +14"6;
8.Duval +21"4... FIA Prod. (14) Rowe +1'24"7

SS22 Bannister South (34,15 km)
1.Loeb 16'00"1; 2.Solberg +1"9; 3.Burns +9"0;
4.Sainz +11"8; 5.C. McRae +12"7;
6.Rovanperä +16"3; 7.Mäkinen +23"3;
8.Hirvonen +34"3... FIA Prod. (13) Rowe +1'36"0

SS23 Bannister West (24,69 km)
1.Solberg 12'22"6; 2.C. McRae +5"5;
3.Sainz +6"0; 4.Mäkinen +6"3; 5.Loeb +9"3;
6.Burns +10"1; 7.Hirvonen +16"6;
8.Duval +21"1... FIA Prod. (15) McShea +1'26"2

SS24 Bannister Central (33,45 km)
1.C. McRae 18'10"0; 2.Sainz +4"0;
3.Solberg +10"9; 4.Hirvonen +13"7;
5.Mäkinen +14"4; 6.Burns +16"6; 7.Loix +23"5;
8.Loeb +29"5... FIA Prod. (15) McShea +1'57"5

Championship Classifications

FIA Drivers (10/14)
1.Burns 55; 2.Solberg 48; 3.Sainz 48; 4.Loeb 45; 5.Grönholm 38; 6.Märtin 37;
7.C. McRae 33; 8.Mäkinen 21; 9.Rovanperä 18; 10.Duval 11; 11.Gardemeister 9;
12.Panizzi 6; 13.Auriol 4; 14.Hirvonen 3; 15.A. McRae 3; 16.Robert 3;
17.Schwarz 3; 18.Tuohino 2; 19.Loix 1; 20.Lindholm 1; 21.Ginley 1

FIA Constructors (10/14)
1.Peugeot 110; 2.Citroën 110; 3.Subaru 74; 4.Ford 61; 5.Skoda 20; 6.Hyundai 12

FIA Junior WRC (4/7)
1.Tirabassi 28; 2.Carlsson 18; 3.Canellas 17; 4.Aava 16; 5.Wilks 15;
6.Katajamäki 10; 7.Ligato 10; 8.Broccoli 9; 9.Svedlund 5; 10.Teuronen 5;
11.Ceccato 4; 12.Cecchettini 4; 13.Feghali 3; 14.Sebalj 3; 15.Baldacci 2; 16.Iliev 2;
17.Harrach 1

FIA Production Car WRC (6/7)
1.Rowe 37; 2.Arai 30; 3.Singh 30; 4.Blomqvist 26; 5.Sola 22; 6.Ligato 13;
7.McShea 8; 8.Al Wahaibi 6; 9.Kulig 6; 10.Roman 6; 11.Trivino 6; 12.Bourne 5;
13.Errani 5; 14.Manfrinato 5; 15.Colsoul 4; 16.De Dominicis 4; 17.Ferreyros 4;
18.Holowczyc 4; 19.Aur 2; 20.Sztuka 2; 21.Marrini 1; 22.Richard 1

Performers

	1	2	3	4	5	6
Solberg	9	9	4	2	-	-
Loeb	9	5	-	5	2	2
Märtin	3	1	7	3	1	-
Grönholm	2	2	1	1	1	-
C. McRae	1	2	2	1	6	5
Duval	1	-	-	-	-	-
Sainz	-	3	2	2	4	2
Mäkinen	-	2	-	3	5	6
Burns	-	-	6	5	2	6
Hirvonen	-	-	1	1	-	-
Rovanperä	-	-	-	3	4	3

Event Leaders

SS1	Solberg
SS2 > SS7	Grönholm
SS8 > SS20	Loeb
SS21	Solberg
SS22	Loeb
SS23 > SS24	Solberg

Previous winners

1989	Kankkunen - Piironen Toyota Celica GT-Four	1996	Mäkinen - Harjanne Mitsubishi Lancer Ev.3
1990	Kankkunen - Piironen Lancia Delta Integrale	1997	McRae - Grist Subaru Impreza WRC
1991	Kankkunen - Piironen Lancia Delta Integrale	1998	Mäkinen - Mannisenmäki Mitsubishi Lancer Ev.5
1992	Auriol - Occelli Lancia Delta HF Integrale	1999	Burns - Reid Subaru Impreza WRC
1993	Kankkunen - Grist Toyota Celica Turbo 4WD	2000	Grönholm - Rautiainen Peugeot 206 WRC
1994	McRae - Ringer Subaru Impreza	2001	Grönholm - Rautiainen Peugeot 206 WRC
1995	Eriksson - Parmander Mitsubishi Lancer Ev.2	2002	Grönholm - Rautiainen Peugeot 206 WRC

Sanremo

Sébastian Loeb scored a dominant victory in the Italian round confirming his status as favourite for the drivers' title. Thanks to his performance Citroën was now alone at the head of the manufacturers ratings despite Panizzi's excellent second place after a last-minute charge.

strada sprovvista
di protezione a valle

WRC
FIA WORLD RALLY
CHAMPIONSHIP

In the dry Gilles Panizzi was slow. When it rained at the end of the rally he chose the right tyres and climbed up to 2nd behind Loeb.

This time Tommi Mäkinen's goodbye tour passed though Italy and the little villages of San Remo. Next year the Italian round will be in Sardinia.

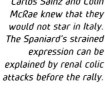

Carlos Sainz and Colin McRae knew that they would not star in Italy. The Spaniard's strained expression can be explained by renal colic attacks before the rally.

THE RALLY
Banco at San Remo

Although an indispensable part of rallying statistics should never be used as a yardstick against which to compare the drivers' art. Sébastian Loeb led the eleventh round of the world championship from start to finish demonstrating flair, the rage to win and was gifted that little piece of luck that often makes the difference between success and failure. Before the start he was extremely wary of Markko Märtin and rightly so. The Estonian and his boss at Ford Malcolm Wilson plus Christian

Loriaux, the Focus's designer, had all being saying that the car would win at least one asphalt rally this season. They were not wrong but forgot the fact that leaves fall in October. The blue oval machine with its open-mouthed front and its very low ground clearance collected them by the rake full at the start of the rally! They clogged the air intake and the efficiency of the fans prevented them from blowing off. The result was that the engine management system detected the inevitable overheating caused by all this debris and went into safety mode reducing power considerably. Thus, neither Märtin nor

Duval was able to set very quick times in the first 2 stages and conceded 20 and 27 secs respectively to the leader Sébastien Loeb after only 39 kilometres. It was infuriating for the Ford no.1 as he had been the only one to able to match the Frenchman's pace according to the times posted in the splits. In the very first service park on the sea front at Imperia not far from the city of flowers the Ford engineers did a good job of improving the air circulation. However, the Fords had lost a lot of time. Having got rid of the leaves Märtin went hell for leather to catch Loeb. He won the next two stages Cosio 1 and San Bartolemeo 1

while the Alsatian hit back by setting scratch times in the final ones of the first leg. When the cars came back to San Remo on Friday 3rd October the Ford driver was 32 seconds behind the Citroën. His determination, though, was intact and his driving during this the first day was of the highest calibre. Fate struck him a cruel blow on the morrow before his car had even made it to the start. Just when he was about to leave the service park the engine stopped dead due to an electronic problem. The time it took to change the ECU located under the driver's seat so as to lower the centre of gravity to the maximum cost him

The Focus's spoiler acted as a snowplough picking up leaves which did not stop Markko from driving a great rally. Even if he could not fight off Panizzi he still finished on the rostrum.

Didier Auriol drove his guts out but the Skoda was not quick enough and following the withdrawal of the Hyundaïs it was the slowest of the WRCs.

Guy Fréquelin travelled to the specials by helicopter and saw his team taking over the lead in the Manufacturers' Championship.

once he had the car set up to his liking he said that the Peugeot was no longer on a par with the Ford or Xsara in terms of performance. The reasons? The 206 at the end of its development was beginning to show its age as the twilight of its career approached. The Peugeot Sport management was not very happy with his comments because it seemed incapable of admitting that its car was no longer the best on asphalt even though it was obvious. The third member of the team, Marcus Grönholm, who was now a good enough all-rounder to win on this surface drove his heart out and was the only one capable of getting anywhere near Loeb and Märtin. Even so he ended the day almost 50 seconds behind the leading pair, a big gap in a tarmac rally. In the Citroën camp neither Sainz nor McRae was able to match the pace of their team-mate. However, the Spaniard had an excuse as two days before the reconnaissance he had undergone an

three minutes and three minutes' lateness equalled a 30 second penalty according to the regulations. "The next time I'll put it on the roof," quipped the Belgian engineer! It was a cruel blow and despite all his panache (a total of 7 scratch times) proved fatal to his chances of victory. Loeb was too far in front. Loeb-Märtin, Märtin-Loeb flashed on the timing screens. One could have been fooled into thinking there were only two drivers in the rally. Obviously it was not the case but the intensity of their duel and their complete commitment eclipsed the rest of the field starting with the Peugeots.

The 206s were completely out-classed on a surface where they had once dominated. Richard Burns drove his usual calculating race and looked so slow that one had to ask oneself whether or not he stopped in each village to do a little business! The leader of the world championship was left way behind and seemed to be a pale shadow of his former self. Gilles Panizzi stated straight away that he was very disappointed with the handling of his car. He soon dropped the new settings and bit-by-bit went back to the basics to which he was accustomed losing precious seconds in the process. What was worse was that

Colin McRae was again behind Carlos Sainz. His past San Remo victories were but a present memory.

François Duval was under extreme pressure from his boss Malcolm Wilson and could do no better than a disappointing 5th place.

It was Cedric Robert's third finish in the top 10 with the same result as in Germany. He deserves a works drive from Peugeot.

operation in Madrid for renal colic. Philippe Bugalski, who was entrusted with a works Xsara, drove a very cautious race on his return to international rallying a year after a big shunt in the 2002 San Remo event. Others to hit problems during the first leg were Toni Gardemeister (accident) and Petter Solberg who ran out of petrol, an error that his team tried to disguise as an electrical fault!

The second leg saw Citroën dominate helped by the penalty inflicted on Märtin early on. The Ford driver then reeled off an impressive series of scratch times in an attempt to catch his rival but in vain. There were no major changes in the order on the second day apart from Panizzi's comeback as he snatched fifth from Duval and Burns's laborious climb from eleventh to ninth place! It was during the final leg that the classification was turned upside down. During the night of Saturday/Sunday the Italian Riviera was hit by strong winds, which flattened the canvas village housing the Junior

Championship. In its wake came dark clouds swollen with rain. Despite this all the crews left the service park before the final stage on slicks except one: Panizzi. "In the worst case you lose a place but on the other you never know," said Jean-Pierre Nicolas to his driver. And he was right. The storm broke and road conditions became completely unsuitable for dry weather tyres. As if to emphasize this the 2-wheel drive cars in the Junior Championship set excellent times and the Italian amateur Pasquale Tarantino in his Clio Williams was second quickest! It was a doddle for Panizzi shod with intermediates. For example, in the 21,52 km Colle d'Oggia stage he was 1m 16.7s quicker than Loeb and above all 1m 28.9s faster than Märtin. In just a couple of sections the king of the asphalt had recaptured his former glory and was up to second place overall. "If we'd had the time to hand groove them I'd have won" laughed Panizzi at the finish not too disappointed and delighted that his gamble had paid off. Had he managed to snatch victory from Loeb it would

have been a travesty of justice as the Alsatian had driven such an intelligent, well-judged rally. Märtin, however, was very unhappy with his third place on the rostrum. Others who scored points were Sainz, Duval, McRae, Burns and Bugalski. Grönholm again did not finish as he was caught out in the final stage and ripped off one of the wheels of his 206, which caused his retirement. Another French driver Nicolas Bernardi won the Super 1600 category. It was a second tricolour double thanks to Simon Jean-Joseph's second place. The winner was a member of the FFSA team and was at the wheel of an Oreca prepared Clio. Not only did he finish thirteenth but he also beat two stars Simon Jean-Joseph and Piero Liatti come out of retirement to drive a 206 in which he really enjoyed himself. This performance came at exactly the right time for Bernardi, the former winner of the Young Rally Talent Trophy, as he was one of the most promising French drivers whose career had been in the doldrums for two years. On the other hand the San Remo rally was a setback for Brice

Richard Burns emerged from obscurity only at the end of the rally. He passed Philippe Bugalski and Cédric Robert scoring 2 points and hanging on to the drivers' title lead.

Bugalski was entered for San Remo by Guy Fréquelin with the express task of taking points from Richard Burns. He stayed ahead of the Englishman until the last special.

Tarabassi's hopes. He arrived in Italy determined to open up a gap in the World Junior Championship for which neither Bernardi, Jean-Joseph nor Liatti was entered but retired at the end of the first leg when his electronics went haywire. Italian Mirco Baldacci in his Fiat Punto scored an unexpected victory from Spanish driver Salvador Canellas (Suzuki). This result enabled the latter to slip past Daniel Carlsson whose Suzuki retired following an accident, into second bringing him to within 3 points of Tirabassi in the championship. With Loeb, Panizzi, Bernardi, Jean-Joseph and Tirabassi it could not be said that France lacked rally drivers.

THE WINNER
Loeb favourite

Following his performance in Australia and with 3 rallies on asphalt coming up a lot of the pundits saw in Sébastien Loeb the favourite for the drivers' title including his team-mates Sainz and McRae. This put a lot of psychological pressure of the shoulders of the young Frenchman, who, it must be remembered, was in his first full season in the world championship. It did not seem to bother him overmuch as he wore a smile at the start despite a heavy cold. After the finish his position as favourite was strengthened even more thanks to his marvellous performance that combined speed, strategy and lucidity. The only reason he was not the championship leader was because Richard Burns had managed to score 2 points by passing Bugalski at the very end of the rally. Carlos Sainz's steadiness also brought him to within spitting distance of the Englishman while the big losers were Grönholm and Solberg who left Italy empty-handed.

In the manufacturers' title chase Citroën added 15 points to its total thanks to Loeb and Sainz as against Peugeot's eleven and retook the overall lead in the championship, which it had lost in New Zealand. There were only five firms entered in Italy as Hyundaï had thrown in the sponge following a financial dispute with MSD the British company responsible for tuning the Accents. The Korean make was talking about a return in 2005 after an in-depth reorganisation but this remains to be seen. As for the San Remo, run for the forty-fifth time, it was its world championship swan's song and it is not expected to return to the calendar being replaced by an event on gravel in Sardinia in 2004. This decision was officialised two weeks later during the Tour of Corsica. ■

Marcus Grönholm was the only one to go off hitting a rock in the last rain-soaked special losing valuable points for Peugeot.

Sébastien Loeb again drove a perfect race on tarmac. He might have been in trouble had the final stage been 10 kilometres longer.

11th Leg of the 2003 World Rally Championship for constructors and drivers. 5th leg of WRC Junior Championship.

Date: 1st to 5th October 2003

Route

1376 km divided in three legs
14 special stages on tarmac (387,28 km)

1st leg

Friday 3rd October (06h30-20h13):
Sanremo > Imperia > Sanremo, 551 km;
6 special stages (142,09 km)

2nd leg

Saturday 4th October (07h00-19h20):
Sanremo > Imperia > Sanremo, 491 km;
4 special stages (149,07 km)

3rd leg

Sunday 5th October (07h00-15h30):
Sanremo > Imperia > Sanremo, 334 km;
4 special stages (96,12 km)

Entry List - Starters - Finishers

63 - 54 - 36

Conditions

Friday: fogy; Saturday: dry weather; Sunday: dry, rain for the last two special stages.

Results — WRC

	Driver/Navigator	Car	Gr.	Time
1	Loeb - Elena	Citroën Xsara WRC	A	4h16'33"7
2	Panizzi - Panizzi	Peugeut 206 WRC		+28"3
3	Märtin - Park	Ford Focus RS WRC 03		+54"6
4	Sainz - Marti	Citroën Xsara WRC		+2'33"2
5	Duval - Prevot	Ford Focus RS WRC 03		+3'58"9
6	C. McRae -Ringer	Citroën Xsara WRC		+4'23"8
7	Burns - Reid	Peugeut 206 WRC		+7'09"5
8	Bugalski - Chiaroni	Citroën Xsara WRC		+7'12"6
9	Robert - Bedon	Peugeut 206 WRC		+7'25"7
10	Mäkinen - Lindstrom	Subaru Impreza WRC03		+7'32"2
11	Baldacci - Bernacchini	Fiat Punto Super 1600	Jr.	+26'48"9

Leading Retirements (18)

	Driver/Navigator	Car		
ES14	Grönholm - Rautiainen	Peugeot 206 WRC		Accident
ES7	Carlsson - Andersson	Suzuki Ignis Super 1.6		Accident
CH6A	Tirabassi - Renucci	Renault Clio 16V		Electronics
CH6A	Solberg - Mills	Subaru Impreza WRC 2003		Out of fuel
ES4	Hirvonen - Lehtinen	Ford Focus RS WRC 02		Engine
ES2	Gardemeister - Lukander	Skoda Fabia WRC		Accident

Special Stage Times

SS1 Perinaldo I (12,39 km)
1.Loeb 7'56"2; 2.Duval +0"5;
3.Grönholm +1"3; 4.Panizzi +1"4;
5.Sainz +2"5; 6.Solberg +5"6;
7.C. McRae +6"1; 8.Märtin +7"2...
Jr. (19) Tirabassi +45"9

SS2 Ceppo I (36,41 km)
1.Loeb 24'05"5; 2.Grönholm +14"7;
3.Duval +20"1; 4.Märtin +20"5;
5.Sainz +24"6; 6.C. McRae +29"0;
7.Panizzi +31"8; 8.Solberg +38"9...
Jr. (17) Baldacci +2'28"5

SS3 Cosio I (19,19 km)
1.Märtin 11'56"3; 2.Loeb +5"0;
3.Panizzi/Duval +5"7;
5.Grönholm +8"8; 6.C. McRae +11"6;
7.Burns +13"9; 8.Solberg +15"0...
Jr. (17) Tirabassi +1'23"6

SS4 S. Bartolomeo I (25,30 km)
1.Märtin 14'47"2; 2.Loeb +1"2;
3.Panizzi +8"9; 4.Grönholm +10"1;
5.Duval +14"7; 6.C. McRae +15"8;
7.Sainz +16"0; 8.Solberg +16"1...
Jr. (17) Baldacci +1'32"9

SS5 Perinaldo II (12,39 km)
1.Loeb 7'45"6; 2.Märtin +0"5;
3.Grönholm +4"6; 4.Panizzi +5"2;
5.Sainz +5"6; 6.Duval +7"3;
7.C. McRae +10"0; 8.Bulgalski +10"8...
Jr. (17) Baldacci +51"6

SS6 Ceppo II (36,41 km)
1.Loeb 23'38"7; 2.Märtin +10"4;
3.Grönholm +16"3; 4.Sainz +16"9;
5.C. McRae +35"6; 6.Duval +36"9;
7.Panizzi +42"8; 8.Solberg +43"1...
Jr. (17) Baldacci +3'10"9

SS7 Teglia I (52,29 km)
1.Märtin 35'01"7; 2.Loeb +0"7;
3.Grönholm +17"3; 4.Panizzi +22"4;
5.Sainz +23"4; 6.Duval +29"8;
7.C. McRae +36"0; 8.Bugalski +41"2...
Jr. (17) Ceccato +4'04"7

SS8 Cosio II (19,19 km)
1.Märtin 11'51"3; 2.Panizzi +6"0;
3.Grönholm +6"3; 4.Duval +6"5;
5.Sainz +7"9; 6.Bugalski +9"1;
7.Loeb +9"6; 8.C. McRae +12"4...
Jr. (16) Cannelas +1'24"5

SS9 S. Bartolomeo II (25,30 km)
1.Märtin 14'44"2; 2.Loeb +2"0;
3.Grönholm +4"1; 4.Panizzi +4"6;
5.Sainz +5"9; 6.Duval +7"9;
7.Bugalski +10"7; 8.Burns +12"4...
Jr. (16) Baldacci +1'37"8

SS10 Teglia II (52,29 km)
1.Märtin 34'48"6; 2.Loeb +6"9;
3.Sainz +9"5; 4.Grönholm +12"4;
5.Panizzi +15"7; 6.Bugalski +32"5;
7.Duval +39"8; 8.C. McRae +41"0...
Jr. (17) Baldacci +4'06"0

SS11 Vignai I (26,54 km)
1.Loeb 18'00"7; 2.Märtin +3"5;
3.Duval +6"8; 4.Sainz +6"9;
5.Grönholm +7"5; 6.Panizzi +11"7;
7.C. McRae +16"5; 8.Burns +18"9...
Jr. (14) Baldacci +2'14"5

SS12 Colle d'Oggia I (21,52 km)
1.Märtin 13'58"7; 2.Grönholm +5"1;
3.Sainz +5"7; 4.Loeb +6"4;
5.Duval +6"9; 6.Panizzi +8"9;
7.Bugalski +15"8; 8.Burns +15"9...
Jr. (13) Baldacci +59"4

SS13 Vignai II (26,54 km)
1.Panizzi 19'42"6; 2.Grönholm +20"0;
3.Loeb +28"3; 4.Märtin +30"4;
5.Bernardi +50"5; 6.Sainz +1'01"8;
7.Duval +1'02"0; 8.C. McRae +1'03"9...
Jr. (18) Canellas +2'03"0

SS14 Colle d'Oggia II (21,52 km)
1.Panizzi 15'59"6; 2.Tarantino +17"3;
3.Bernardi +51"2; 4.Higgins +52"3;
5.Liatti +54"5; 6.Corona +1'02"9;
7.Joges +1'14"2; 8.Burns/Loeb +1'16"7...
Jr. (11) Feghali +1'21"7

Championship Classifications

FIA Drivers (11/14)
1.Burns 57; 2.Loeb 55; 3.Sainz 53; 4.Solberg 48; 5.Märtin 43; 6.Grönholm 38;
7.C. McRae 36; 8.Mäkinen 21; 9.Rovanperä 18; 10.Duval 15; 11.Panizzi 14;
12.Gardemeister 9; 13.Auriol 4; 14.Hirvonen 3; 15.A. McRae 3; 16.Robert 3;
17.Schwarz 3; 18.Tuohino 2; 19.Bugalski 1; 20.Ginley 1; 21.Lindholm 1; 22.Loix 1

FIA Constructors (11/14)
1.Citroën 125; 2.Peugeot 121; 3.Subaru 76; 4.Ford 71; 5.Skoda 21; 6.Hyundai 12

FIA Junior WRC (5/7)
1.Tirabassi 28; 2.Canellas 25; 3.Carlsson 18; 4.Wilks 18; 5.Aava 16; 6.Baldacci 12;
7.Katajamäki 10; 8.Ligato 10; 9.Teuronen 10; 10.Broccoli 9; 11.Iliev 8;
12.Cecchettini 8; 13.Svedlund 5; 14.Feghali 5; 15.Ceccato 4; 16.Sebalj 3;
17.Harrach 1

FIA Production Car WRC (6/7)
1.Rowe 37; 2.Arai 30; 3.Singh 30; 4.Blomqvist 26; 5.Sola 22; 6.Ligato 13;
7.McShea 8; 8.Al Wahaibi 6; 9.Kulig 6; 10.Roman 6; 11.Trivino 6; 12.Bourne 5;
13.Errani 5; 14.Manfrinato 5; 15.Colsoul 4; 16.De Dominicis 4; 17.Ferreyros 4;
18.Holowczyc 4; 19.Aur 2; 20.Sztuka 2; 21.Marrini 1; 22.Richard 1

Performers

	1	2	3	4	5	6
Märtin	7	3	-	2	-	-
Loeb	9	5	1	1	-	-
Panizzi	2	1	2	4	1	2
Grönholm	-	3	6	2	2	-
Duval	-	1	3	1	2	4
Tarantino	-	1	-	-	-	-
Sainz	-	-	2	2	6	1
Bernardi	-	-	1	-	1	-
Higgins	-	-	-	1	-	-
C. McRae	-	-	-	-	1	3
Liatti	-	-	-	-	1	-
Bugalski	-	-	-	-	-	2
Solberg	-	-	-	-	-	1
Corona	-	-	-	-	-	1

Event Leaders

SS1 > SS14　　Loeb

Previous winners

1973	Thérier - Jaubert Alpine Renault A110		1989	Biasion - Siviero Lancia Delta Integrale
1975	Waldegaard - Thorszelius Lancia Stratos		1990	Auriol - Occelli Lancia Delta Integrale
1976	Waldegaard - Thorszelius Lancia Stratos		1991	Auriol - Occelli Lancia Delta Integrale
1977	Andruet - Delferrier Fiat 131 Abarth		1992	Aghini - Farnocchia Lancia Delta HF Integrale
1978	Alen - Kivimaki Lancia Stratos		1993	Cunico - Evangelisti Ford Escort RS Cosworth
1979	Fassina - Mannini Lancia Stratos		1994	Auriol - Occelli Toyota Celica Turbo 4WD
1980	Rohrl - Geistdorfer Fiat 131 Abarth		1995	Liatti - Alessandrini Subaru Impreza
1981	Mouton - Pons Audi Quattro		1996	McRae - Ringer Subaru Impreza
1982	Blomqvist - Cederberg Audi Quattro		1997	McRae - Grist Subaru Impreza WRC
1983	Alen - Kivimaki Lancia Rally 037		1998	Mäkinen - Mannisenmäki Mitsubishi Lancer Evo 5
1984	Vatanen - Harryman Peugeot 205 T16		1999	Mäkinen - Mannisenmäki Mitsubishi Lancer Evo 6
1985	Rohrl - Geistdorfer Audi Sport Quattro S1		2000	Panizzi - Panizzi Peugeot 206 WRC
1986	Alen - Kivimaki Lancia Delta S4		2001	Panizzi - Panizzi Peugeot 206 WRC
1987	Biasion - Siviero Lancia Delta HF 4WD		2002	Panizzi - Panizzi Peugeot 206 WRC
1988	Biasion - Siviero Lancia Delta Integrale			

Mirco Baldacci

France

Petter Solberg in his
Subaru scored his first
win on asphalt helped
by his Pirellis that were
perfectly adapted to the
tricky road conditions
His task was made
easier by Loeb and
Märtin's errors and his
victory put him right
back in the drivers' title
chase

Marcus Grönholm
saw the finish in
4th place snatched
from Colin McRae.
The Peugeots were
slowed by a bad
choice of tyre.

Helped by his
Pirellis and his
skill Peter Solberg
won his first rally
on asphalt.

THE RALLY
A first for Solberg

Petter Solberg really had to dig deep into his resources to win this event. The day before the rally he had a big accident that destroyed his car and also gave him one hell of a scare. A driver has to have a lot of self-confidence and fearlessness to set off again in a car that has been totally rebuilt. Over the past few years two of the older stars, Tommi Mäkinen and Colin McRae, have never really recovered from serious crashes and one of the explanations for their fall off in pace could be the after-effects of their big shunts. The Norwegian had neither record nor title to his name so there was no question of soft-pedalling. The car was so badly damaged that his presence at the start looked compromised. So what were the alternatives? Bring over a

Carlos Sainz's 2nd place put him into the lead for the drivers' world title, which Burns had occupied for 8 months. He was 3 points ahead of Solberg and Loeb.

It was another nightmare rally for Skoda. Didier Auriol did not even start (electronics) in an event where he had achieved some of his most notable exploits. Gardemeister (here) was bedevilled by problems.

car from England? Ask Mäkinen to relinquish his seat? The Finn did indeed offer to let Petter take over his car but finally after a night's work for the mechanics (and a sleepless one for Solberg) the team managed to rebuild his Impreza thanks to the help provided by the local Subaru dealer in Ajaccio. However, when he turned up for the start of the first stage in a car whose bodywork still bore traces of its misadventure on its left-hand side few specialists gave him a chance of winning apart from a handful of enlightened Italian journalists, Guido Rancatti and Andrea Cordovani, who skilfully analysed the situation and bet on Pirelli.

On dry asphalt the Italian rubber is no match Michelin, winner for the past 5 years of all the rallies run on this type of surface. If it rains heavily the French tyres still have a slight advantage but when the roads are damp and greasy or alternate dry and very wet sections the Pirellis are much superior thanks to a tyre designed specially for Monte Carlo. This soft tyre has deep grooves and Subaru has such confidence in it that the team immediately fits this type of rubber when rain threatens. All one has to do is to analyse the Norwegian's progress to understand the determining role played by the tyres. In the first stage in the dry he could do no

One can almost see the steam coming from Elena and Loeb's ears. Sébastian went off on Saturday morning and lost 10 minutes as the Xsara stopped astride a bank.

Tyres played a capital role and the Pirellis have been better than the Michelins in the wet for quite some time and it was an unusually wet Corsican event.

better than eighth 43 secs behind the leader, Sébastian Loeb. In the second the rain had just fallen, very heavily in places, leaving the roads very slippery, ideal conditions for the Pirelli-shod Subaru. He certainly benefited from errors committed by Loeb and Märtin but did not make any mistakes. At the end of the leg he set 3 scratch times- his only three in the rally-and overtook Duval who was a little too inexperienced to fight him off. How Loeb and Märtin would have reacted is a moot question. Once Solberg was in front he controlled his lead very cleverly and in the final leg nursed his car to his first victory on asphalt. The young coming men-Loeb, Märtin and

Solberg whose average age in 28-are skilled all-round drivers. The second has not yet won on asphalt and the third has not done so on gravel but in both cases success will not be long in coming.

The winner took advantage of errors made by the Citroën and Ford drivers both of whom began the French round as the bookies' favourites but it was Carlos Sainz who set the first scratch time. The Spaniard's lead was short-lived as Märtin went to the front after the second stage proving the speed of the Ford and its driver on asphalt. Before the start of the rally the Frenchman and the Estonian were

touted as hot favourites for the drivers' title and they knew that it was not by adopting Burns' tactics that they would win the championship. However, second time through Cargese the Ford spun losing 25 secs and the lead to the Citroën. François Duval in the other Focus set the fastest time in the special putting him in second place. Märtin had not given up although at the end of the first leg he was fifth 18.5 secs behind the leader who had Duval, Grönholm and Sainz hot on his heels. During the early stages Alexandre Bengué in a private 206 WRC made a big impression as he set excellent times during the day

including a blinding fourth quickest through Vico second time round, better than all the works cars! He could have a brilliant future and even though he destroyed his Peugeot in the first special on the second day his performance did not go unnoticed. France does not lack talent. However, one of its old stagers, Didier Auriol, never even got to the start of the rally due to electronic problems in the Skoda's gearbox management system.

Day two looked like being a difficult one. Heavy rain had fallen during the night in the Ajaccio region and showers still threatened. In these conditions tyre choice was as important as it was tricky. The observers in the specials, the weather forecasters in the teams, the men

François Duval was in first place on the evening of the 2nd day after Loeb's off. He finally finished 3rd, his second rostrum after Turkey.

This was Markko Märtin's most error-strewn rally on the season. He went off once a day and for good on the third in an accident that left him with a painful neck.

Colin McRae again finished bagging 3 points, not enough to leave him in with a shout for the title. But Colin's mind was on 2004.

responsible for hand-cutting the tyres, engineers, drivers and team managers were all in a quandary. In the first special, Ampaza, a shower fell a few kilometres from the finish as the three leaders flashed through. It was during the second that the outcome of the rally was decided. Markko Märtin, author of the quickest time in SS1 and Loeb both made mistakes. The Estonian broke a rim and Sébastien spun. His Xsara ended up with its front wheels in the sand and the rear ones hanging over a drop. The Ford lost 5 minutes and the Citroën ten the time it took for enough spectators to arrive and get him back on the road again. This dropped both drivers way down the time sheets and seriously compromised their world championship chances. "It's a black day," moaned the Estonian. "I've lost any chance of winning in Corsica and it's a big blow to my title hopes." He restarted in a very disappointed frame of mind, set mediocre times and crashed out on the third day.

Loeb, though, did not give up and was quickest in all the stages of the last leg proving that he could have fought off Solberg in his Pirelli-shod Subaru. For the record the scratch time in the Pont de Masina special that sounded the death knell of the Frenchman and the Estonian's hopes was set by Mikko Hiroven, his first in the world championship thanks to a judicious choice of mixed tyres. The young Finn, who was the first to admit how surprised he was at his performance, showed a fine turn of speed on a surface that he barely knew.

With Loeb having fallen back to eighteenth place François Duval took over the lead. The young Belgian drove as best he could but was unable to stay ahead of Solberg in his Pirelli-shod Subaru. The next day he lost second place to Carlos Sainz who benefited from a cunning choice of tyres by his team and was the only Michelin driver to shod slicks for the last two specials. He shot back up the classification making full use of his rubber. Taking such risks is the true hallmark of a champion. His second place put him into the lead in the Drivers' Championship ahead of Solberg, Burns (who scored one point) and Loeb. In the manufacturers' classification Citroën increased its advance over Peugeot. The performance of the reigning Manufacturers' Championship leader was yet again very disappointing. Grönholm (fourth) and Panizzi (sixth) did all they could despite haphazard tyre choices but it was obvious that the 206 had come to the end of the road. In addition to Subaru, Ford or Citroën could have won the rally, which never even looked likely for Peugeot. It was time for the 206's retirement!

Alexandre Begué drove a magnificent rally in his 206 until he tore a wheel off. The young Frenchman won his home championship on asphalt this year.

Tommi Mâkinen is a great sportsman. After the shakedown he offered Prodrive the use of his Subaru for Solberg who had destroyed his own.

Gilles Panizzi drove an unimpressive rally on the asphalt as he was not happy with his car. Grönholm beat him for once on tarmac and he finished 6th.

Petter Solberg nearly lost everything during the shakedown and his start appeared compromised. This is what his Impreza looked like after hitting a pylon. An all-nighter by the mechanics fixed things.

FIA PRODUCTION
Rowe champion

Will winning the Production World Championship title give a boost to Martin Rowe's career? It is not a foregone conclusion when one remembers that it didn't open any doors for the more recent Group N champions Karamjit Singh from Malaysia, Argentinean Gabriel Pozzo and Manfred Stohl from Austria. When the Englishman arrived in Corsica for the last round his aim was very simple. If his closest challenger Toshihiro Araï retired all he had to do was finish fifth to clinch the title. As the Japanese has never really been at home on asphalt Rowe's task did not look too difficult.

Retirements fell thick and fast including that of Dani Sola, particularly good on tarmac. As the specials unfolded Araï got closer and closer to Niall McShea from Ireland who emerged winner of the French round of the FIA Production Championship although the best Group N driver was Mike Higgins. The Japanese finished second and Rowe third which was good enough to give him the title. It was the 32-year-old Englishman's first international success before which his best result was victory in the 1998 British Championship in a Renault Maxi Megane. Maybe he was not the most brilliant driver during the year as he had scored only one win like Kulig from Poland, Sola and McShea compared with Araï's three but he was the steadiest.

This season saw Subaru's revenge in the FIA Production Championship. For the last few years the Japanese manufacturer's performance in Group N had been overshadowed by that of archrival Mitsubishi due to a lack of investment. This year the policy was much more ambitious thanks to the arrival of the new Impreza and in addition Mitsubishi was losing interest in this cup which had virtually evolved into a one make competition. Since 1995 it had won every time either in its own name or as in 2002 with Proton, one of its satellite brands. Last year Singh's Pert was just a Lancer in disguise. In the Production Championship Subaru scored 4 victories to Mitsubishi's three and the former's first title was won with the help of Rowe and tuner David Sutton. It will certainly not be the last! ∎

Englishman, Martin Rowe, the season's Mr. Steady, won the Production Cars' World title (Group N) in his Mitsubishi.

139

12th Leg of the 2003 World Rally Championship for constructors and drivers. 7th FIA Production Car WRC Championship.

Date: 15th to 19th October 2003

Route
971,75 km divided in three legs
16 special stages on tarmac
(397,30 km)

1st leg
Friday 17th October (09h05-17h14):
Ajaccio > Ajaccio, 283,03 km;
6 special stages (95,28 km)

2nd leg
Saturday 18th October (07h15-19h28):
Ajaccio > Ajaccio, 447,60 km;
6 special stages (189,96 km)

3rd leg
Sunday 19th October (07h00-14h30):
Ajaccio > Ajaccio, 240,92 km;
4 special stages (112,06 km)

Entry List - Starters - Finishers
71 - 62 - 34

Conditions
Friday: dry weather;
Saturday and Sunday: rain.

Results $\quad$ WRC

	Driver/Navigator	Car	Gr.	Time
1	**Solberg - Mills**	**Subaru Impreza WRC 2003**	**A**	**4h20'15"3**
2	Sainz - Marti	Citroën Xsara WRC		+36"6
3	Duval - Prevot	Ford Focus RS WRC 03		+41"7
4	Grönholm - Rautiainen	Peugeot 206 WRC		+1'09"2
5	C. McRae - Ringer	Citroën Xsara WRC		+1'26"0
6	Panizzi - Panizzi	Peugeot 206 WRC		+1'58"7
7	Mäkinen - Lindstrom	Subaru Impreza WRC 2003		+2'25"8
8	Burns - Reid	Peugeot 206 WRC		+2'36"7
9	Bugalski - Chiaroni	Citroën Xsara WRC		+2'46"8
10	Hirvonen - Lehtinen	Ford Focus RS WRC 02		+3'55"4
16	**McShea - Patterson**	**Mitsubishi Lancer Evo 7**	**Prod.**	**+29'32"5**

Leading Retirements (28)

ES15	Märtin - Park	Ford Focus RS WRC 03	Accident
ES11	Stohl - Minor	Peugeut 206 WRC	Accident
ES10	Rousselot - Mondesir	Subaru Impreza	Accident
ES7	Bengue - Escudero	Peugeut 206 WRC	Accident
ES1	Auriol - Giraudet	Skoda Fabia WRC	Electronics

TOP ENTRIES

1 Marcus GRÖNHOLM - Timo RAUTIAINEN Peugeot 206 WRC
2 Richard BURNS - Robert REID Peugeot 206 WRC
3 Gilles PANIZZI - Hervè PANIZZI Peugeot 206 WRC
4 Markko MÄRTIN - Michael PARK Ford Focus RS WRC 03
5 Francois DUVAL - Stèphane PREVOT Ford Focus RS WRC 03
6 Mikko HIRVOVEN - Jarmo LEHTINEN Ford Focus RS WRC 02
7 Petter SOLBERG - Philip MILLS Subaru Impreza WRC 2003
8 Tommi MÄKINEN - Kaj LINDSTROM Subaru Impreza WRC 2003
14 Didier AURIOL - Denis GIRAUDET Skoda Fabia WRC
15 Toni GARDEMEISTER - Paavo LUKANDER Skoda Fabia WRC
17 Colin McRAE- Derek RINGER Citroën Xsara WRC
18 Sébastien LOEB - Daniel ELENA Citroën Xsara WRC
19 Carlos SAINZ - Marc MARTI Citroën Xsara WRC
20 Philippe BUGALSKI - Jean-Paul CHIARONI Citroen Xsara
21 Alexandre BENGUE - Caroline ESCUDERO Peugeut 206 WRC
22 Anthony WARMBOLD - Gemma PRICE Ford Focus WRC 02
24 Cedric ROBERT - Gerald BEDON Peugeot 206 WRC
32 Manfred STOHL - Ilka MINOR Peugeot 206 WRC
34 Benoit ROUSSELOT - Gilles MONDESIR Subaru Impreza
35 Alistair GINLEY - Rory KENNEDY Ford Focus WRC
52 Daniel SOLA - Alex ROMANI Mitsubishi Carisma Evo 7
53 Ramon FERREYROS - Javier MARIN Mitsubishi Lancer Evo 7
54 Toshihiro ARAI - Tony SIRCOMBE Subaru Impreza
55 Martin ROWE - Trevor AGNEW Subaru Impreza
58 Marco LIGATO - Ruben GARCIA Mitsubishi Lancer Evo 7
59 Stefano MARRINI - Titiana SANDRONI Mitsubishi Lancer Evo 7
60 Niall McSHEA - Chris PATTERSON Mitsubishi Lancer Evo 6
61 Janusz KULIG - Maciej SZCEPANIAK Mitsubishi Lancer
64 Joakim ROMAN - Ragnar SPJUTH Mitsubishi Lancer Evo 5
65 Stig BLOMQVIST - Ana GONI Subaru Impreza WRX STI
69 Bob COLSOUL - Tom COLSOUL Mitsubishi Lancer
70 Riccardo ERRANI - Stefano CASADO Mitsubishi Lancer
72 Titi AUR - Adrian BERGHEA Mitsubishi Lancer Evo 7
77 Alfredo DE DOMINICIS - Giovanni BERNACCHINI Mitsubishi Lancer Evo 7
101 Brice TIRABASSI - Jacques JULIEN RENUCCI Renault Clio Ragnotti

Special Stage Times

SS1 Cargese I (14,64 km)
1.Sainz 9'49"6; 2.Burns +0"9;
3.Märtin +1"6; 4.C. McRae +1"9;
5.Grönholm +2"2; 6.Duval +2"4
7.Loeb +2"7; 8.Solberg +6"6...
FIA Prod. (22) Kulig +1'09"7

SS2 Vico I (15,48 km)
1.Loeb 10'04"6; 2. Märtin +0"8;
3.Grönholm +1"6; 4.Sainz +2"5;
5.Duval +3"1; 6.Solberg +3"4;
7.Burns +6"0; 8.C. McRae +8"8...
FIA Prod. (20) Sola +53"7

SS3 Golfe De La Liscia I (17,52 km)
1.Märtin 10'43"6; 2.Loeb +3"1;
3.Sainz +5"0; 4.Burns +5"4;
5.Grönholm +5"6; 6.Solberg +8"4;
7.Duval +9"7; 8.C. McRae 12"5...
FIA Prod. (21) Sola +1'10"2

SS4 Cargese II (14,64 km)
1.Duval 9'45"3; 2.Grönholm +3"6;
3.Loeb +4"3; 4.C. McRae +5"8;
5.Sainz +6"9; 6.Panizzi +7"7;
7.Bugalski +7"9; 8.Burns +9"2...
FIA Prod. (19) Sola +49"3

SS5 Vico II (15,48 km)
1.Märtin 10'03"6; 2.Loeb +2"6;
3.Duval +3"0; 4.Bengue +3"8;
5.Grönholm +4"7; 6.Burns +6"4;
7.C. McRae +8"1; 8.Sainz +8"5...
FIA Prod. (19) Sola +50"4

SS6 Golfe De La Liscia II (17,52 km)
1.Märtin 10'43"2; 2.Duval +0"5;
3.Loeb/Sainz +2"1; 5.Grönholm +2"4;
6.Burns +6"4; 7.C. McRae +7"1;
8.Bugalski +8"7...
FIA Prod. (21) Sola +1'07"9

SS7 Ampazza I (38,63 km)
1.Märtin 25'32"2; 2.Solberg +4"4;
3.Loeb +8"9; 4.Sainz +13"0;
5.Panizzi +13"1; 6.Duval +15"4;
7.C. McRae 21"7; 8.Bugalski 25"9...
FIA Prod. (18) Sola +2'30"3

SS8 Pont De La Masina I (15,42 km)
1.Hirvonen 10'31"5; 2.Loeb +8"5;
3.Gardemeister +9"2; 4.Panizzi +9"7;
5.Robert +11"4; 6.Mäkinen +15"4;
7.Solberg +16"4; 8.Burns +19"4...
FIA Prod. (15) Sola +1'20"6

SS9 Col De Carazzi I (40,93 km)
1.Panizzi 27'23"5; 2.Loeb +1"8;
3.Duval +7"4; 4.Sainz +8"4;
5.Grönholm +17"0; 6.Solberg +18"5;
7.Hirvonen +18"8; 8.Gardemeister +28"9...
FIA Prod. (19) Sola +2'37"6

SS10 Ampaza II (38,63 km)
1.Solberg 25'20"7; 2.Märtin +12"9;
3.Sainz +13"4; 4.Duval +19"9;
5.Panizzi +22"8; 6.C. McRae +24"8;
7.Hirvonen/Mäkinen +28"3...
FIA Prod. (16) Sola +2'24"1

SS11 Pont De La Masina II (15,42 km)
1.Solberg 10'22"3; 2.Märtin +3"2;
3.Duval +3"3; 4.Sainz +6"0
5.C. McRae +8"5; 6.Burns +9"9;
7.Hirvonen +10"4; 8.Mäkinen +11"2...
FIA Prod. (15) McShea +1'14"3

SS12 Col De Carazzi II (40,93 km)
1.Solberg 27'15"6; 2.Mäkinen +9"2;
3.Märtin +17"6; 4.Sainz +17"8;
5.Loeb +18"0; 6.C. McRae +18"8;
7.Duval +21"1; 8.Hirvonen +21"8...
FIA Prod. (16) Sola +2'52"8

SS13 Penitencier Coti Chiavari I (24,23 km)
1.Loeb 15'19"0; 2.Solberg +3"3;
3.Duval +7"6; 4.Grönholm +9"6;
5.Mäkinen +10"6; 6.Sainz +10"7;
7.C. McRae +11"9; 8.Panizzi +13"6...
FIA Prod. (18) Arai +1'45"6

SS14 Pont De Calzola I (31,80 km)
1.Loeb 19'47"2; 2.Solberg +4"7;
3.Grönholm +6"3; 4.Panizzi +6"7;
5.Burns +11"1; 6.Sainz +11"5;
7.Mäkinen 12"6; 8.Bugalski +13"3...
FIA Prod. (17) Arai +2'14"6

SS15 Penitencier Coti Chiavari II (24,23 km)
1.Loeb 15'25"4; 2.Grönholm +0"6;
3.C. McRae +1"8; 4.Solberg +6"7;
5.Duval/Bugalski +8"7;
7.Burns +10"6; 8.Panizzi +11"4...
FIA Prod. (16) Kulig +1'46"4

SS16 Pont De Calzola II (31,80 km)
1.Loeb 19'56"4; 2.Grönholm +2"8;
3.Sainz +6"5; 4.Bugalski +7"9;
5.Mäkinen +10"9; 6.Burns +11"4;
7.Robert +14"4; 8.C. McRae +15"7...
FIA Prod. (15) Kulig +2'17"2

Championship Classifications

FIA Drivers (12/14)
1.Sainz 61; 2.Solberg 58; 3.Burns 58; 4.Loeb 55; 5.Grönholm 43; 6.Märtin 43;
7.C. McRae 40; 8.Mäkinen 23; 9.Duval 21; 10.Rovanperä 18; 11.Panizzi 17;
12.Gardemeister 9; 13.Auriol 4; 14.Robert 3; 15.A. McRae 3; 16.Schwarz 3;
17.Hirvonen 3; 18.Tuohino 2; 19.Bugalski 1; 20.Ginley 1; 21.Lindholm 1; 22.Loix 1

FIA Constructors (12/14)
1.Citroën 137; 2.Peugeot 129; 3.Subaru 88; 4.Ford 78; 5.Skoda 21; 6.Hyundai 12

FIA Junior WRC (5/7)
1.Tirabassi 28; 2.Canellas 25; 3.Carlsson 18; 4.Wilks 18; 5.Aava 16; 6.Baldacci 12;
7.Katajamäki 10; 8.Ligato 10; 9.Teuronen 10; 10.Broccoli 9; 11.Iliev 8;
12.Cecchettini 8; 13.Svedlund 5; 14.Feghali 5; 15.Ceccato 4; 16.Sebalj 3;
17.Harrach 1

FIA Production Car WRC (7/7)
1.Rowe 43; 2.Arai 38; 3.Blomqvist 30; 4.Singh 30; 5.Sola 22; 6.McShea 18;
7.Ligato 13; 8.Kulig 11; 9.Trivino 8; 10.Colsoul 7; 11.Al Wahaibi 6; 12.Roman 6;
13.Errani 6; 14.Bourne 5; 15.Manfrinato 5; 16.De Dominicis 4; 17.Ferreyros 4;
18.Holowczyc 4; 19.Aur 2; 20.Sztuka 2; 21.Marrini 1; 22.Richard 1

Performers

	1	2	3	4	5	6
Loeb	5	3	3	-	1	-
Märtin	4	3	2	-	-	-
Solberg	3	3	-	1	-	3
Duval	1	1	4	1	2	2
Sainz	1	-	4	5	1	2
Panizzi	1	-	-	2	2	1
Hirvonen	1	-	-	-	-	-
Grönholm	-	3	2	1	5	-
Burns	-	1	-	1	1	4
C. McRae	-	-	1	2	1	2
Bugalski	-	1	-	1	1	-
Mäkinen	-	1	-	-	2	1
Gardemeister	-	-	1	-	-	-
Bengue	-	-	-	1	-	-
Robert	-	-	-	1	-	-

Event Leaders

SS1	Sainz
SS2 > SS3	Märtin
SS4 > SS7	Loeb
SS8 > SS11	Duval
SS12 > SS16	Solberg

Previous winners

1973	Nicolas – Vial Alpine Renault A 110	1988	Auriol – Occelli Ford Sierra RS Cosworth
1974	Andruet – "Biche" Lancia Stratos	1989	Auriol – Occelli Lancia Delta Integrale
1975	Darniche – Mahé Lancia Stratos	1990	Auriol – Occelli Lancia Delta Integrale
1976	Munari – Maiga Lancia Stratos	1991	Sainz – Moya Toyota Celica GT-Four
1977	Darniche – Mahé Fiat 131 Abarth	1992	Auriol – Occelli Lancia Delta HF Integrale
1978	Darniche Mahé Fiat 131 Abarth	1993	Delecour – Grataloup Ford Escort RS Cosworth
1979	Darniche – Mahé Lancia Stratos	1994	Auriol – Occelli Toyota Celica Turbo 4WD
1980	Thérier – Vial Porsche 911SC	1995	Auriol – Giraudet Toyota Celica GT-Four
1981	Darniche – Mahé Lancia Stratos	1996	Bugalski – Chiaroni Renault Maxi Megane
1982	Ragnotti – Andrié Renault 5 Turbo	1997	McRae – Grist Subaru Impreza WRC
1983	Alen – Kivimaki Lancia Rally 037	1998	McRae – Grist Subaru Impreza WRC
1984	Alen – Kivimaki Lancia Rally 037	1999	Bugalski – Chiaroni Citroën Xsara Kit Car
1985	Ragnotti – Andrié Renault 5 Turbo	2000	Bugalski – Chiaroni Peugeot 206 WRC
1986	Saby – Fauchille Peugeot 205 T16	2001	Puras – Marti Citroën Xsara WRC
1987	Béguin – Lenne BMW M3	2002	Panizzi – Panizzi Peugeot 206 WRC

España

Gilles Panizzi snatched victory right at the end of the rally after an incredible tyre gamble as the choice of rubber played a crucial role in the outcome of the event. Sébastian Loeb's second place made him joint leader of the Drivers' World Championship with his team-mate Carlos Sainz.

WRC
FIA WORLD RALLY
CHAMPIONSHIP

"Each time I'm in the lead, it rains!" Sébastian Loeb was able to keep his 1st place in Italy but could do nothing about Panizzi in Spain after dominating the rally.

Richard Burns looked much more at home than in the 2 previous rallies. He retired after hitting a rock and breaking his suspension.

The teams change but Sainz is as popular as ever in Spain whatever the colours.

THE RALLY
Panizzi gets the rubber right

It was a thrilling rally up to the very last second with Panizzi pipping Loeb as the finish approached. Gilles was in top form and his pleasure was apparent for all to see. It was a great battle and could be summed up by sayings like: 'He who laughs last laughs longest,' 'catch as catch can,' or the 'Tortoise and the Hare!' Technology, though, is generally a fairly humourless business and often has little to do with great drivers expressing the perfect mastery of their art so to understand Panizzi's feat it is necessary to have a look at the tyre story. When the cars set off on the first leg it looked as if they would have to tackle dry but very cold asphalt. The air was icy and the countryside around Vic white with frost. So there were two words on everybody's lips, Monte Carlo the only

possible comparison with this autumn battle. The Pirelli-shod Subarus were immediately reduced to the role of outsider as the Italian rubber only comes into its own on damp, patchy surfaces. This effectively reduced the battle for victory to the teams fitted with Michelins each one making its own choice. Panizzi opted for cold surface tyres, as did Burns even if his rubber was a little less specific. Grönholm after a little hesitation went for the same choice as Panizzi who was the quickest on asphalt in the team. Citroën and Ford both chose Code 2 Michelins for intermediate road temperatures. Their choice was spot on, as the first leg with three timed stages scheduled and no tyre changes allowed proved merciless. Loeb, winner of two out of the 3 specials-Solberg having won the very short first stage before falling back-went straight into the lead

Marcus Grönholm was handicapped from the start by a wrong tyre choice. He scored 3 points for his team after his least competitive rally on the year.

We are not on the roads of the 'Tour de France' for cyclists but on those of the Catalonia rally. An unlucky Sainz suffered from engine cut outs at the end.

Markko Märtin fitted with the right tyres like Panizzi at the end of the rally and again finished on the rostrum. On day 1 he was still complaining of pains in his neck after his violent crash in Corsica.

opening up an incredible gap of 25 seconds over Burns. Panizzi lost 38.1 secs to the Citroën and Grönholm totally at sea was down in fourteenth place 1m 22.8s behind the leader. Only Sainz (second 9.5secs behind) Solberg and Märtin both 20 secs further back managed to hang onto the Frenchman. The Ford driver's performance was an excellent one considering that he was in great pain after his accident at the end of the Tour of Corsica. Gloom pervaded the Peugeot camp as its direct adversary for the Manufacturers' Championship racked up the wins. In addition, the seconds lost would be very hard to pull back as Loeb was at his brilliant best and was really going for it. He was helped by the fact that Petter Solberg, one of his direct rival for the drivers' title, received a 50 second penalty on the exit from a service park as his mechanics had taken 5 minutes too long to change the alternator on his Subaru.

Towards the end of the first leg Gilles Panizzi, who now had the right tyres, launched his charge. He set 2 scratch times and climbed from eighth to fourth place. He returned to Lloret de Mar 33.5 secs behind the leader. There were no changes in the first three places. On the morrow Markko Märtin in much better form than the previous day went into maximum attack mode, as he was more determined than ever to win his first rally on asphalt. He was good enough, had the right car for the surface and was in with a real chance. However, try as he might he soon realised just how difficult it was to make up time on dry tarmac. Over 8 specials totalling some 131 kilometres in which he set 3 scratch times he could only pull back 10.4 secs on Loeb. Panizzi on the other hand was a bit erratic and lost 3 seconds to the leader. He managed to slip past Sainz into second place, the latter not being able to set up his Xsara to his liking.

The second Ford works driver François Duval showed that his Corsican performance was no flash in the pan. He was among the front-runners in fifth and on asphalt the blue oval team could not have had a better back up driver. A very disenchanted Didier Auriol did not make it back to Lloret de Mar. His Skoda retired due to clutch failure in the first stage of the day. On the evening of the second leg the rally had lost a lot of its suspense as it was impossible to see how Loeb could be caught and most people now accepted that the Alsatian's victory was inevitable. The weather decided otherwise.
"As soon as I lead a rally it rains," said Loeb with a slight grimace at the start of the third leg. As in Australia and in Italy showers appeared on Sunday morning. Just the right kind of weather for the Subarus to make their come back. Solberg and Mäkinen were in their element and each set a scratch time as soon as the cars were

François Duval was again well placed finishing 4th only just over half-a-minute behind his team leader. His future at Ford still looks doubtful.

Bad communication between Citroën and Michelin probably sealed Loeb's fate as his team was not told about tyres that were better in heavy rain.

Petter Solberg got away lightly. On the first day he was penalised 50 secs (prolonged alternator change) putting him outside the points. He came home 5th thanks to the rain and the late mishaps affecting Sainz and Burns.

unleashed. In his last season the 4-times world champion proved that he had lost none of his skills on the 35 km Viladrau stage on soaking wet roads. The teams shod by Michelin were in trouble except for Kresta in his private 206 entered by the Bozina team who set a scratch time taking advantage of his starting position. Third quickest in the Viladrau stage won by Mäkinen Grönholm conceded 40 secs, Loeb 46 and Panizzi 52. It was just a temporary hiccup was the general opinion as the overall classification remained more or less

unchanged except that Solberg was now back in the points, a moral boost for the Norwegian in his pursuit of the world title.

In fact, the rally was far from over as Loeb quickly realised in the early part of the second-last special no.20. He had chosen rain tyres that were too hard and he would have to make do with them until the end. This time it was Citroën that botched things and the Subaru-Pirelli tandem had got it right. Michelin had produced a few 'magic' tyres but only Ford and

It was the end of a sequence of 3 points scoring finishes for McRae. After announcing he would take a year off he battled against the soon-to-retire Mäkinen.

Skoda in the wars: The clutch went on Auriol's car and Toni Gardemeister's martyrdom continued.

Peugeot knew about them. These tyres had been designed for Monte Carlo and their softness really worked miracles for the cars' grip. Straight off Märtin, Grönholm and Panizzi banged in three scratch times. Gilles really let it all hang out and in 51 kilometres pulled back his 50 seconds deficit on Loeb and increasing the gap by 13 secs just to add insult to injury. His final charge was all the more incredible as at the start of the last stage his main aim was defending his position in the overall classification. His team quickly realised that he was

about to pull off a spectacular success and gave him to the Go Faster signal. He did and won his seventh world championship rally.

Sébastian Loeb's expression on the rostrum spoke volumes about how disappointed he was. He had not only lost victory but also 2 crucial points in the race for the title because of tyres he was unaware of. "I knew nothing about those mixed tyres with soft rubber. I was hardly aware of their existence. Given my situation I didn't want to take risks

Tommi Mäkinen showed his old flair. He set his first scratch time since Cyprus in June.

Loeb was the quickest in the rally. Despite the upset in the classification in the final stage he went to Great Britain dead heating with Carlos Sainz (but leading in terms of wins) and one point ahead of Petter Solberg.

by fitting them." Peugeot did and played its cards well leaving Catalonia with 13 points as against Citroën's 10. This had not happened since Argentina and the Lion had been dominated by its sister company for 7 rallies. Before the final shoot out in Great Britain the arithmetic was simple: Peugeot had to claw back 5 points. Difficult but not impossible.

In the drivers' classification the results of the 39th Catalonia Rally ratcheted the suspense up another notch. Loeb and Sainz were joint leaders as the Spaniard had scored the 2 points awarded for seventh position despite an engine problem that lost him 3 places in the final special when he was in fourth spot. Only one point behind these two came Petter Solberg fifth in Catalonia and then Burns 5 points further back. As the teams left Spanish soil all eyes now turned to Great Britain.

THE JUNIORS
Tirabassi strengthens his hold

The Spanish rally was the scene of the second-last round in the 2003 Junior Championship. Brice Tirabassi in the lead decided to base his strategy on the performance of his most dangerous rival Salvador Canellas. Although the Spaniard knew the roads in Catalonia better than the Renault driver he was never really a threat as his Suzuki was just that little bit slower on asphalt than the Clio, and his skills were not a match for those of the reigning French rally champion. In the first leg the latter opened up a gap of one minute and then decided to control his lead. He won the Junior event from Kris Meeke in his Opel and finally Canellas could do no better than third. Thus, Tirabassi returned to his

native Var after a fairly uneventful rally 7 points ahead of the Spaniard, a big advantage with only one rally to go. However, the above-mentioned were not the quickest over the whole rally and victory in the Super 1600 Category went to the inevitable Simon Jean-Joseph in his Clio. Brice never really tried to carry the fight to the man from Martinique as his main aim was to dishearten Canellas but nonetheless Jean-Joseph scored a remarkable win. He was helped by Nicolas Bernardi's accident in the last stage of the second leg as up to then the Italian, winner of his national 1600 championship, had been in the lead. The French drivers' double in their Renault Clios reinforced the tricolour's grasp on world rallying in the wake of Panizzi and Loeb in cars made in France. Just to rub salt into the wound they were all on Michelin tyres! ∎

Brice Tirabassi won the second-last round putting him in an ideal position in the Junior Championship. The Renault driver was in the lead before going to Wales.

Fabulous Gilles Panizzi. He scored a win on his last rally in a works 206 Peugeot with a little help from Lady Luck. He was given a triumphant reception by his team.

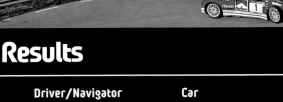

39th Rally of Spain - Catalunya

13th Leg of the 2003 World Rally Championship for constructors and drivers. 6th leg of WRC Junior Championship.

Date: 22nd to 26th October 2003

Route
1553,72 km divided in three legs
22 special stages on tarmac
(381,10 km)

1st leg
Friday 24th October (06h45-21h03):
Lloret > Vic > Lloret, 654,07 km;
8 special stages (146,32 km)

2nd leg
Saturday 25th October(07h00-18h08):
Lloret > Vic > Lloret, 429,69 km;
8 special stages (131,22 km)

3rd leg
Sunday 26th October (05h30-15h09):
Lloret > Vic > Lloret, 429,69 km;
6 special stages (103,56 km)

Entry List - Starters - Finishers
51 - 47 - 33

Conditions
Friday and Saturday: dry weather;
Sunday: heavy rain.

Results — WRC

	Driver/Navigator	Car	Gr.	Time
1	**Panizzi - Panizzi**	**Peugeut 206 WRC**	A	**3h55'09"4**
2	Loeb - Elena	Citroën Xsara WRC		+13"0
3	Märtin - Park	Ford Focus RS WRC 03		+13"6
4	Duval - Prevot	Ford Focus RS WRC 03		+55"4
5	Solberg - Mills	Subaru Impreza WRC 2003		+1'10"8
6	Grönholm - Rautiainen	Peugeut 206 WRC		+1'29"1
7	Sainz - Marti	Citroën Xsara WRC		+1'43"0
8	Mäkinen - Lindstrom	Subaru Impreza WRC 2003		+1'55"1
9	C. McRae - Ringer	Citroën Xsara WRC		+3'15"2
10	Bugalski - Chiaroni	Citroën Xsara WRC		+5'13"6
11	Robert - Bredon	Peugeot 206 WRC		+5'28"1
12	Gardemeister - Lukander	Skoda Fabia WRC		+5'58"2
17	**Tirabassi - Renucci**	**Renault Clio 1.6 16v**	Jr.	**+21'24"3**

Leading Retirements (14)

		Car	
ES22	Warmbold - Price	Ford Focus WRC 02	Machanical prob.
ES19	Burns - Reid	Peugeut 206 WRC	Accident
ES9	Auriol - Giraudet	Skoda Fabia WRC	Clutch

TOP ENTRIES

1. Marcus GRÖNHOLM - Timo RAUTIAINEN Peugeot 206 WRC
2. Richard BURNS - Robert REID Peugeot 206 WRC
3. Gilles PANIZZI - Hervè PANIZZI Peugeot 206 WRC
4. Markko MÄRTIN - Michael PARK Ford Focus RS WRC 03
5. Francois DUVAL - Stèphane PREVOT Ford Focus RS WRC 03
6. Mikko HIRVOVEN - Jarmo LEHTINEN Ford Focus RS WRC 02
7. Petter SOLBERG - Philip MILLS Subaru Impreza WRC 2003
8. Tommi MÄKINEN - Kaj LINDSTROM Subaru Impreza WRC 2003
14. Didier AURIOL - Denis GIRAUDET Skoda Fabia WRC
15. Toni GARDEMEISTER - Paavo LUKANDER Skoda Fabia WRC
17. Colin McRAE- Derek RINGER Citroën Xsara WRC
18. Sébastien LOEB - Daniel ELENA Citroën Xsara WRC
19. Carlos SAINZ - Marc MARTI Citroën Xsara WRC
20. Philippe BUGALSKI - Jean-Paul CHIARONI Citroën Xsara WRC
21. Cedric ROBERT - Gerald BEDON Peugeut 206 WRC
22. Roman KRESTA - Jan TOMANEK Peugeut 206 WRC
23. Antony WARMBOLD - Gemma PRICE Ford Focus WRC 02
33. Alistair GINLEY - Rory KENNEDY Ford Focus WRC
51. Mirco BALDACCI - Giovanni BERNACCHINI Fiat Punto Super 1600
52. Daniel CARLSSON - Mattias ANDERSSON Suzuki Ignis Super 1600
54. Kosti KATAJAMÄKI - Jani LAAKSONEN Volkswagen Polo
57. Dimitar ILIEV - Yanaki YANAKIEV Peugeot 206 WRC
61. Brice TIRABASSI - Jacques JULIEN RENUCCI Renault Clio 1.6 16V
62. Oscar SVEDLUND - Bjöm NILSSON Volkswagen Polo
63. Massimo CECCATO - Mitia DOTTA Fiat Punto
64. Ville-Perti TEURONEN - Harri KAAPPARO Suzuki Ignis Super 1600
65. Abdo FEGHALI - Joseph MATAR Ford Puma
67. Alessandro BROCCOLI - Giovanni AGNESE Opel Corsa Super 1600
69. Salvador CANELLAS - Xavier AMIGO Suzuki Ignis Super 1600
70. Guy WILKS - Phil PUGH Ford Puma
71. Urmo AAVA - Kuldar SIKK Suzuki Ignis Super 1600
73. Krum DONCHEV - Rumen MANOLOV Peugeot 206 Super 1600
74. Kris MEEKE - Chris PATTERSON Opel Corsa Super 1600
76. Luca CECCHETTINI - Marco MUZZARELLI Fiat Punto Super 1600
101. Simon JEAN-JOSEPH - Jacques BOYERE Renault Clio 1.6

Special Stage Times

www.rallycatalunya.com
www.wrc.com

SS1 La Trona I (13,17 km)
1.Solberg 8'23"6; 2.Duval +0"1;
3.Märtin +0"3; 4.Loeb +1"8;
5.Panizzi +2"8; 6.C. McRae +3"1;
7.Burns +3"2; 8.Sainz +3"4...
Jr. (24) Tirabassi +50"8

SS2 Alpens-Les Liosses (21,79 km)
1.Loeb 13'07"3; 2.Sainz +4"5;
3.Märtin+6"9; 4.C. McRae +9"1;
5.Burns +10"5; 6.Solberg +14"3;
7.Mäkinen +15"5; 8.Panizzi 19"1...
Jr. (24) Tirabassi +1'25"6

SS3 Le Pobla de Lillet I (22,54 km)
1.Loeb 15'03"5; 2.Sainz +3"4;
3.Solberg +7"5; 4.Burns +13"5;
5.C. McRae +14"8; 6.Märtin +15"5
7.Mäkinen +17"3; 8.Panizzi +18"0...
Jr. (23) Tirabassi +1'34"3

SS4 Sant Julia I (26,27 km)
1.Loeb 15'35"3; 2.Panizzi +0"5;
3.Duval +1"8; 4.Sainz +2"5;
5.Märtin +3"0; 6.Burns +4"5;
7.Grönholm +10"2; 8.C. McRae +15"5...
Jr. (24) Canellas +1'47"6

SS5 Taradell I (5,05 km)
1.Märtin 2'56"2; 2.Panizzi/Sainz +1"2;
4.Loeb +2"2; 5.Burns +2"3; 6.Duval +2"4;
7.Grönholm/Solberg +4"4...
Jr. (22) Meeke +20"6

SS6 La Trona I (13,17 km)
1.Panizzi 8'15"7; 2.Märtin +2"9;
3.Duval +3"1; 4.Burns +4"5;

5.Loeb +5"0; 6.Sainz +7"1;
7.Grönholm +8"4; 8.Solberg 9"0...
Jr. (23) Tirabassi +51"2

SS7 Alpens - Les Losses II (21,79 km)
1.Panizzi 13'10"6; 2.Duval +1"0;
3.Loeb +1"3; 4.Märtin +3"4;
5.Sainz +5"9; 6.Bugalski +7"1;
7.Grönholm +7"5; 8.Solberg 12"4...
Jr. (19) Tirabassi +1'13"0

SS8 La Ploba de Lillet II (22,54 km)
1.Loeb 14'55"3; 2.Panizzi +2"2;
3.Burns +5"6; 4.Bugalski +7"9;
5.Duval +8"2; 6.Sainz +8"5;
7.Märtin +9"5; 8.Grönholm +11"4...
Jr. (18) Tirabassi +1'36"2

SS9 Olost I (23,07 km)
1.Panizzi 11'39"4; 2.Märtin +0"5;
3.Loeb +2"3; 4.Duval +4"7;
5.Grönholm +8"1; 6.Burns +10"6;
7.C. McRae +13"2; 8.Solberg +13"8...
Jr. (20) Meeke +1'13"3

SS10 Lluca I (14,03 km)
1.Märtin 8'15"9; 2.Duval +0"2;
3.Burns +2"6; 4.Panizzi +2"9;
5.Loeb +3"2; 6.Sainz +6"1;
7.Bugalski +6"6; 8.Grönholm +6"7...
Jr. (22) Canellas +51"7

SS11 Sant Boi de Llucanes (12,85 km)
1.Panizzi 8'06"7; 2.Märtin/Loeb +0"5;
4.Burns +2"5; 5.Duval +3"5;
6.Solberg +4"2; 7.Sainz +4"8;
8.C.McRae +5"9... Jr. (21) Tirabassi +48"7

SS12 Sant Julia II (26,27 km)
1.Duval 15'30"4; 2.Panizzi +0"7;
3.Grönholm +1"0; 4.Loeb +2"8;
5.Märtin/C. McRae +5"0;
7.Solberg + 5"9; 8.Burns +6"2...
Jr. (20) Tirabassi +1'37"3

SS13 Taradell II (5,05 km)
1.Burns 2'58"3; 2.Märtin +0"1;
3.Sainz +0"5; 4.Panizzi +0"7;
5.Solberg/Loeb +0"8;
7.Grönholm +0"9; 8.Robert +1"2...
Jr. (17) Meeke +16"3

SS14 Olost II (23,07 km)
1.Märtin 11'37"0; 2.Loeb +3"4;
3.Grönholm +4"9; 4.Panizzi +6"2;
5.Duval +7"1; 6.Burns +10"0;
7.Sainz +11"3; 8.C. McRae +13"7...
Jr. (21) Tirabassi +1'13"4

SS15 Lluca II (14,03 km)
1.Märtin 8'19"5; 2.Duval +2"2;
3.Sainz +3"9; 4.Solberg +4"4;
5.Loeb +5"1; 6.Robert +5"7;
7.Burns +7"1; 8.Grönholm +7"4...
Jr. (23) Teuronen +49"4

SS16 Sant Boi de Llucanes II (12,85 km)
1.Loeb 8'05"5; 2.Märtin +1"6;
3.Panizzi +1"9; 4.Duval +2"9;
5.Grönholm +3"0; 6.Sainz +4"6;
7.Solberg +5"5; 8.Burns +5"9...
Jr. (19) Tirabassi +49"9

SS17 Sant Bartomeu del Grau I (11,55 km)
1.Solberg 6'27"2; 2.Mäkinen +2"2;
3.Sainz +16"5; 4.Grönholm +16"9;

5.C. McRae +18"4; 6.Loeb +18"7;
7.Märtin +21"9; 8.Duval +22"5...
Jr. (16) Canellas +36"2

SS18 La Roca I (5,05 km)
1.Kresta 3'16"2; 2.Mäkinen +3"2;
3.Solberg +3"6; 4.Panizzi +5"1;
5.Burns/Sainz +5"5;7.Loeb +5"8;
8.C. McRae +6"8... Jr. (18) Tirabassi +18"9

SS19 Viladrau I (35,18 km)
1.Mäkinen 23'19"8; 2.Solberg +6"9;
3.Grönholm +40"5; 4.Loeb +46"6;
5.Panizzi +52"1; 6.C. McRae +53"6;
7.Sainz +1'03"2; 8.Duval +1'06"9...
Jr. (17) Tirabassi +2'09"6

SS20 Sant Bartomeu del Grau II (11,55 km)
1.Märtin 6'29"4; 2.Solberg +2"6;
3.Duval +4"2; 4.Mäkinen +5"3;
5.Panizzi +6"0; 6.Sainz +7"6;
7.Grönholm +8"0; 8.Gardemeister +10"3...
Jr. (16) Tirabassi +34"8

SS21 La Roca II (5,05 km)
1.Grönholm 3'22"2; 2.Duval +0"2;
3.Panizzi +0"8; 4.Gardemeister +1"3;
5.Robert +2"0; 6.Kresta +2"6;
7.Sainz +2"8; 8.Solberg +3"4...
Jr. (16) Tirabassi +17"5

SS22 Viladrau II (35,18 km)
1.Panizzi 23'38"4; 2.Grönholm +0"8;
3.Märtin +3"3; 4.Duval +12"3;
5.Mäkinen +18"6; 6.Solberg +22"1;
7.Gardemeister +22"7; 8.Loeb +44"0...
Jr. (17) Tirabassi +2'06"7

Championship Classifications

FIA Driver (13/14)
1.Loeb 63; 2.Sainz 63; 3.Solberg 62; 4.Burns 58; 5.Märtin 49; 6.Grönholm 46;
7.C. McRae 40; 8.Panizzi 27; 9.Duval 26; 10.Mäkinen 24; 11.Rovanperä 18;
12.Gardemeister 9; 13.Auriol 4; 14.Robert 3; 15.A. McRae 3; 16.Schwarz 3;
17.Hirvonen 3; 18.Tuohino 2; 19.Ginley 1; 20.Lindholm 1; 21.Loix 1; 22.Bugalski 1

FIA Constructors (13/14)
1.Citroën 147; 2.Peugeot 142; 3.Subaru 93; 4.Ford 89; 5.Skoda 21; 6.Hyundai 12

FIA Junior WRC (6/7)
1.Tirabassi 38; 2.Canellas 31; 3.Carlsson 23; 4.Aava 20; 5.Wilks 18;
6.Teuronen 13; 7.Baldacci 12; 8.Katajamäki 10; 9.Ligato 10; 10.Broccoli 9;
11.Cecchettini 8; 12.Iliev 8; 13.Meeke 8; 14.Feghali 7; 15.Ceccato 5;
16.Svedlund 5; 17.Sebalj 3; 18.Harrach 1

FIA Production Car WRC (7/7)
1.Rowe 43; 2.Arai 38; 3.Blomqvist 30; 4.Singh 30; 5.Sola 22; 6.McShea 18;
7.Ligato 13; 8.Kulig 11; 9.Trivino 8; 10.Colsoul 7; 11.Al Wahaibi 6; 12.Roman 6;
13.Errani 6; 14.Bourne 5; 15.Manfrinato 5; 16.De Dominicis 4; 17.Ferreyros 4;
18.Holowczyc 4; 19.Aur 2; 20.Sztuka 2; 21.Marrini 1; 22.Richard 1

Performers

	1	2	3	4	5	6
Märtin	5	5	3	1	2	1
Panizzi	5	4	2	4	3	-
Loeb	5	2	2	4	4	1
Solberg	2	2	2	1	1	3
Duval	1	5	3	3	3	1
Mäkinen	1	2	-	1	1	-
Grönholm	1	1	3	1	2	-
Burns	1	-	2	3	2	4
Kresta	1	-	-	-	-	-
Sainz	-	3	3	1	2	5
C. McRae	-	-	-	1	3	2
Bugalski	-	-	-	1	-	1
Gardemeister	-	-	-	1	-	-
Robert	-	-	-	-	1	1

Event Leaders

SS1	Solberg
SS2 > SS21	Loeb
SS22	Panizzi

Previous winners

1991	Schwarz - Hertz Toyota Celica GT-Four	1997	Mäkinen - Harjanne Mitsubishi Lancer Ev.4
1992	Sainz - Moya Toyota Celica Turbo 4WD	1998	Auriol - Giraudet Toyota Corolla WRC
1993	Delecour - Grataloup Ford Escort RS Cosworth	1999	Bugalski - Chiaroni Citroën Xsara Kit Car
1994	Bertone - Chiapponi Toyota Celica Turbo 4WD	2000	C. McRae - Grist Ford Focus WRC
1995	Sainz - Moya Subaru Impreza	2001	Auriol - Giraudet Peugeot 206 WRC
1996	McRae - Ringer Subaru Impreza	2002	Panizzi - Panizzi Peugeot 206 WRC

Great Britain

All the suspense that had been built up by the battles for both the drivers' and manufacturers' titles evaporated early on following the retirements of Sainz, Grönholm and Märtin. Richard Burns did not even make it to the start after collapsing a week before the event. Petter Solberg won the drivers award helped by Citroën's decision to order Loeb lift off to ensure the manufacturers title, the main aim of Peugeot's sister company.

Sébastian Loeb, Daniel Elena and Carlos Sainz have a good laugh. This was before the rally. Sainz's retirement on Friday morning spelt the end of his team-mate's title chances.

Petter Solberg made his intentions clear right from the start knowing he had to beat the Citroën drivers, and went into the lead after the 1st super special in Cardiff.

Sébastian Loeb was yet again mind-boggling. He dominated drivers like Tommi Mäkinen and Colin McRae while he was supposed to control his race which upped the pressure on him.

François Duval made no mistakes in this tough rally. His Ford Focus never missed a beat unlike Markko Märtin's and he finished 5th.

Marcus Grönholm mucked up the end of his season between poor performances and silly mistakes. His contact with a stone sounded the death knell of Peugeot's title hopes.

THE RALLY
To Solberg with thanks from Citroën

"Often races that generate enormous excitement do not fulfil their promise," declared François Chatriot the Citroën Sport team manager who, after his long career as a driver, knew what he was talking about. He said this on the eve of the rally in the bar of the hotel where Citroën had set up its headquarters for the Rally GB. Not too far away Sébastian Loeb and Carlos Sainz reeled off interviews as a large number of journalists especially from France, Spain and Norway had come to Cardiff. The French were all riding on a wave of enthusiasm generated by Loeb in the press, on the radio and TV. Never since the 205 Turbo 16 era in the 80s had there been such interest in rallying. Didier Auriol's title in a Toyota and those of the 206 WRC (with a Finnish driver) had never really succeeded in mobilising the mass media to such an extent. Citroën had no room for error. If there

was such frenzy it was to see the drivers title going to Loeb and not the manufacturers' one to a Xsara WRC. "Let's get the ball rolling right now," exclaimed an excited Chatriot.

The only fly in the ointment was Richard Burns' absence. On Sunday 2nd November the day before the reconnaissance he collapsed at the wheel of his Porsche on his way to Wales. Luckily Markko Märtin was in the car and the Estonian managed to control the ensuing slide and stop the Porsche on the side of the road. The Peugeot driver was immediately rushed to hospital, which he left soon afterwards only to collapse again in his hotel room. The doctors immediately forbade him to take part in the last rally of the year robbing him of the chance of battling for the drivers' title and perhaps scoring a win for Peugeot on his final outing for the team. And so two years of collaboration marked more by misunderstandings than success came to a painful end. In addition it took the doctors a long time to diagnose Burns' problem.

Peugeot expected Harri Rovanperä to carry the fight to the leaders and compensate for Grönholm's early exit. He did neither and his team bosses were far from happy.

Didier Auriol has had a difficult year with Skoda but seems ready to take up the gauntlet for 2004 depending what the team has to offer.

Tommi Mäkinen enjoyed his last rally. He was under no pressure and kept a weather eye on his young team-mate's progress to the drivers' title.

changed down and we went off." Exit one of the three championship pretenders due to an error caused by a camera that had not been tested in the car, as Citroën was not told that it was a new model.

The dramatic consequences of this retirement made themselves felt immediately. Citroën's general manager Claude Satinet, who was in France, telephoned Guy Fréquelin and asked him to tell Loeb to slow down. There were only 2 Xsaras left and they had to finish to ensure victory in the Manufacturers' Championship. This effectively pulled the rug from under Sébastian's feet in his chase for the drivers' title. "We've decided to privilege the manufacturers' title,» said a very downcast Fréquelin. "I really feel for Sébastian but please

With Burns out the battle for the title came down to a shoot-out between Loeb, Sainz and Solberg, the first two dead heating and the third only a point behind. The first Super Special run at night time did not break the deadlock so everybody eagerly awaited the first real special early on Friday morning 7th November. Sébastian Loeb immediately set the two quickest times in the Brechfa and Trawscoed specials ousting Solberg from the lead. However, an incident occurred which was to have a major influence on both the outcome of the rally and the championships just before Carlos Sainz set off. The camera installed in his Xsara's cockpit caught fire. It was a new model specially designed for live transmission of the final stage of the rally. The Spaniard managed to put it out but lost precious time before roaring off his usually rock-solid concentration shattered. "In fact, I wasn't ready," he said afterwards. "I set off but I wasn't concentrated and I didn't listen to what Marc (his co-driver) told me. We came into a long left-hander in sixth instead of third and I didn't even try to brake. I just

Czech Roman Kresta had a good season in his private 206. He set 2 scratch times in Germany and then in Catalonia and should be part of the works Skoda team in 2004.

Citroën boss Claude Satinet's decision to give priority to the manufacturers' title by slowing Loeb made him the target of a lot of flak from the numerous French media present.

Tommi would have liked a final skirmish with Colin McRae but the latter was under Citroën team orders.

understand our position. Citroën is not to blame. You mustn't get things wrong." OK, it was the fire that was responsible for the state of affairs but it was a hurried and rather shortsighted decision by the team, a newcomer to in the world championship. A finer analysis of the rally might have put off or indeed prevented this mind-boggling team order. At that very moment not only was Sainz out but so also were Grönholm and Märtin, two other possible winners, the first due to an accident in Trawscoed and the second with a blown engine. Above all with the Finn out of the way a Citroën victory looked on the cards as most of Peugeot's hopes of closing the gap separating it from its sister company rested on Marcus's shoulders. In addition the other two 206 drivers were way down the field. Harri Rovanperä was in eighth place and Freddy Loix brought in at the last

minute to replace Richard Burns was in tenth. Colin McRae was in a solid fourth position so in fact there was no need for panic in the Citroën camp and thus no reason to order Loeb to hold back. Company logic overcame the sporting aspect. Understandable but very damaging when a team has such a talented and charismatic driver on its payroll. "We didn't sacrifice Loeb," stated Claude Satinet later on playing on words in a rather cynical fashion. "He was not given an order not to be world champion. We just asked him to finish." It was a haggard Guy Fréquelin who had to dash his protégé's dreams; a terrible dilemma for a man who, 22 years earlier, had seen his own world title chances evaporate here in Great Britain when he was beaten by Ari Vatanen. Never again would he find himself in such a position. Loeb obviously has a great future ahead of him but it was a chance not to be missed.

Finally, Citroën forgot that the manufacturers' title generates much less media fallout. Who remembers that Toyota won in 1999 while the victories in the championship of Burns and Grönholm between 2000 and 2002 have made a much bigger

impact than the three titles won by Peugeot in the same period? Loeb is a Citroën employee. End of story!

Once the order had sunk in Sébastian slowed. "He really lifted off in the fourth special," confided his co-driver Daniel Elena. This resulted in a loss of 8.5 secs on Solberg who immediately went into a lead he was never to lose. At that moment the rally more or less fizzled out as the battle for the title was all over bar the shouting. The Subaru driver had an uneventful run to his first crown and his display of unfettered joy once the line had been crossed was a pleasure to see. Loeb kept it between the hedges and finished second in compliance with Citroën's team orders. Afterward Guy Fréquelin and himself kept repeating:" Petter drove an excellent rally. It would have been very hard to beat him." Nobody was fooled. Loeb let the first and second legs go but when Rovanperä retired at the start of the third he was free to push again and won two out of three specials. He was as quick as Solberg and he could have

Freddy Loix called in at the last minute to replace Richard Burns, who had collapsed twice, had only around 100 kms' experience in the 206. He did a good job. Roll on 2004.

After a good opening day the weather was dull for Colin McRae's last outing (provisionally) in his home rally which he has won on 3 occasions plus the championship in 1995.

Toni Gardemeister was hit with mechanical problems throughout the rally and he finally crashed out on the last day. The Skoda Fabia did not show its true potential this year.

won; he could have been champion. Sébastian always finds the right words: "It's not here that we lost the title but in several other places starting with Catalonia because we selected the wrong tyres." Had he not made a bad tyre choice due to the fact that he did not know the full range of Michelin rubber he would have won, arrived in Great Britain with an extra 2 points and been champion. But ifs don't win rallies, or indeed anything else!

Petter Solberg is an excellent world champion and fully deserves his title thanks to his panache and his 4 victories, more than any other driver this year. "It's true that I'd like to have had a longer battle with Sébastian in this rally," he stated at the finish, "but it's a great day for me. I can't find the right words to express what I'm feeling."

Citroën deserved its manufacturers' title won in Great Britain thanks to Loeb and and McRae's fourth despite a puncture. In addition, it broke Peugeot's run of 3 consecutive successes. "Bravo Citroën, "said Corrado Provera. "I have one regret, though. It's that the number 1 attributed to the world champion leaves our 206 and does not go to another French car." The Loeb controversy will be forgotten when the Alsatian is world champion. "We'll do everything to help him," stated his boss Guy Fréquelin on the evening of the Rally GB.

However, France did not leave Wales empty-handed as Brice Tirabassi was crowned Junior Champion. Although the category was won by Carlsson in his Suzuki the Frenchman became champion despite retiring with a blown engine during the second leg because his closest rival Salvador Canellas could do no better than fourth. "I hope to follow in Sébastian's footsteps as he was junior champion two years ago and is now making headlines in the WRC," declared the Renault driver after the rally. He'll need all the help he can get from his fairy godmother!

Sébastian Loeb sportingly acknowledged that Solberg would have been very difficult to beat. With McRae, Burns and now Solberg Pirelli has dominated this rally for almost 10 years.

THE FINAL BOW
Goodbye to the old guard

The no-holds barred battle between Tommi Mäkinen and Colin McRae throughout the rally added a whiff of nostalgia to the event, as it was reminiscent of them in their heyday. However, their times were nearly always slower than those of their successors Petter Solberg and Sébastian Loeb. That's why they're bowing out after what is probably their last world championship event, as they seem incapable of matching the speed of the latest generation of drivers. Obviously getting older, kids at home, accidents etc have all taken their toll on the extraordinary potential they showed in the 90s when they were the top dogs in rallying. The Finn's retirement is final while the Scot is hoping to make a comeback in the not too distant future. They battled for third place behind the young chargers and finally it fell to Mäkinen when McRae's Citroën suffered a puncture in the last special. Tommi Mäkinen was in tears when he made a final appearance at the post-race press conference and his words, full of wisdom and force, moved the journalists present. "I would like to say thank you to you all. The marvellous years I've spent among you and the fans have been incredible. I'm going to miss you all and I think it's going to be very difficult to live far away from all of that next season when Monte Carlo comes round. Thank you again." His speech received a long-standing ovation and one of the most affected was Petter Solberg as they are firm friends. Mäkinen has passed everything on to him, race craft, strategy, settings appointing him as his natural successor. "You've made me go quicker than ever," said the young world champion to his old master. "And this win, Tommi, is for you. "Solberg has everything it takes to become one of the greats like Mäkinen and McRae. ■

What are Tommi Mäkinen and Colin McRae talking about in the Subaru's cockpit? The new generation of unbelievably quick drivers perhaps...?

Results — WRC

	Driver/Navigator	Car	Gr.	Time
1	**Solberg - Mills**	**Subaru Impreza WRC 2003**	**A**	**3h28'58"1**
2	Loeb - Elena	Citroën Xsara WRC		+43"6
3	Mäkinen - Lindstrom	Subaru Impreza WRC 2003		+2'58"8
4	C. McRae - Ringer	Citroën Xsara WRC		+5'28"1
5	Duval - Prevot	Ford Focus RS WRC 03		+7'16"1
6	Loix - Smeets	Peugeot 206 WRC		+8'06"5
7	Stohl - Minor	Peugeot 206 WRC		+8'48"4
8	Kresta - Tomanek	Peugeot 206 WRC		+9'02"6
9	Pykalisto - Mannisenmäki	Peugeot 206 WRC		+9'53"6
10	Latvala - Antilla	Ford Focus RS WRC02		+12'25"3
14	**Carlsson - Andersson**	**Suzuki Ignis**	**Prod.**	**+28'31"7**

Leading Retirements (36)

ES16	Gardemeister - Lukander	Skoda Fabia WRC	Accident
ES16	Rovanperä - Pietilainen	Peugeot 206 WRC	Transmission
ES14	Sola - Romani	Citroën Xsara WRC	Fire
ES11	Tirabassi - Renucci	Renault Clio	Engine
ES8	Panizzi - Panizzi	Peugeot 206 WRC	Transmission
ES4	Märtin - Park	Ford Focus RS WRC 03	Engine
CH3A	Grönholm - Rautiainen	Peugeot 206 WRC	Stopped by police
ES3	Hirvonen - Lehtinen	Ford Focus RS WRC 03	Accident
ES3	Sainz - Marti	Citroën Xsara WRC	Accident

14th and last leg of the 2003 World Rally Championship for constructors and drivers. 7th and last leg of WRC Junior Championship.

Date: 5th to 9th November 2003

Route
1574,52 km divided in three legs
18 special stages on dirt road
(376,80 km)

Superspecial
Thursday 6th Novembre (19h30):
Cardiff (2,45km)

1st leg
Friday 7th November (05h30-20h05):
Cardiff > Felindre > Cardiff, 638,28 km;
7 special stages (164,23 km);

2nd leg
Saturday 8th November (05h00-20h13):
Cardiff > Felindre > Cardiff, 582,62 km;
8 special stages (138,71 km)

3rd leg
Sunday 9th November (05h20-13h24):
Cardiff > Felindre > Cardiff, 363,62 km;
3 special stages (73,86 km)

Entry List - Starters - Finishers
85 - 75 - 39

Conditions
dry weather, fog and mud.

TOP ENTRIES

1	Marcus GRÖNHOLM - Timo RAUTIAINEN Peugeot 206 WRC
2	Freddy LOIX - Sven SMEETS Peugeot 206 WRC
3	Harri ROVANPERÄ - Risto PIETILÄINEN Peugeot 206 WRC
4	Markko MÄRTIN - Michael PARK Ford Focus RS WRC 03
5	Francois DUVAL - Stèphane PREVOT Ford Focus RS WRC 03
6	Mikko HIRVOVEN - Jarmo LEHTINEN Ford Focus RS WRC 03
7	Petter SOLBERG - Philip MILLS Subaru Impreza WRC 2003
8	Tommi MÄKINEN - Kaj LINDSTROM Subaru Impreza WRC 2003
14	Didier AURIOL - Denis GIRAUDET Skoda Fabia WRC
15	Toni GARDEMEISTER - Paavo LUKANDER Skoda Fabia WRC
17	Colin MCRAE- Derek RINGER Citroën Xsara WRC
18	Sébastien LOEB - Daniel ELENA Citroën Xsara WRC
19	Carlos SAINZ - Marc MARTI Citroën Xsara WRC
20	Jari-Matti LATVALA - Mikka ANTILLA Ford Focus RS WRC 02
21	Gilles PANIZZI - Hervè PANIZZI Peugeut 206 WRC
22	Roman KRESTA - Jan TOMANEK Peugeot 206 WRC
23	Antony WARMBOLD - Gemma PRICE Ford Focus WRC
24	Juuso PYKALISTO - Risto MANNISENMÄKI Peugeut 206 WRC
25	Daniel SOLA - Alex ROMANI Citroën Xsara WRC
26	Jan KOPECKY - Filip SCHOVANER Skoda Octavia WRC
27	Steve PEREZ - Jonty BOLSOVER Ford Focus
33	Alistair GINLEY - Rory KENNEDY Ford Focus WRC
34	Manfred STOHL - Ilka MINOR Peugeut 206 WRC
35	Tobias JOHANSSON - Bo HOLMSTRAND Toyota Corolla WRC
37	Andréas ERIKSSON - Per-Ola SVENSSON Ford Focus WRC
38	Tapio LAUKKANEN - Harri KAAPRO Subaru Impreza WRC
51	Mirco BALDACCI - Giovanni BERNACCHINI Fiat Punto
52	Daniel CARLSSON - Mattias ANDERSSON Suzuki Ignis
61	Brice TIRABASSI - Jacques JULIEN RENUCCI Renault Clio
64	Ville-Pertti TEURONEN - Mikko MARKKULA Suzuki Ignis
67	Alessandro BROCCOLI - Giovanni AGNESE Opel Corsa
69	Salvador CANELLAS - Xavier AMIGO Suzuki Ignis
70	Guy WILKS - Phil PUGH Ford Puma
71	Urmo AAVA - Kuldar SIKK Suzuki Ignis
100	Martin ROWE - Chris WOOD Subaru Impreza WRX Sti

Special Stage Times

SS1 Cardiff Super Sp 1 (2,45 km)
1.Solberg 2'08"7; 2.Märtin +1"4;
3.Grönholm/Mäkinen +1"8;
5.Sainz +3"2; 6.Loix/Loeb +3"3;
8.C. McRae +3"5...
FIA Prod. (38) Baldacci +16"3

SS2 Brechfa (23,12 km)
1.Loeb 13'19"6; 2. Solberg +4"6;
3.Märtin +8"4; 4.Grönholm +10"4;
5.Sainz +18"9; 6.Mäkinen +24"6;
7.C. McRae +26"2; 8.Duval +29"8...
FIA Prod. (30) Meeke +2'25"9

SS3 Trawscoed (27,96 km)
1.Loeb 16'23"4; 2.Solberg +2"5;
3.Märtin +5"6; 4.Mäkinen +21"8;
5.C. McRae +31"5; 6.Rovanperä +32"4;
7.Duval/Pykalisto +36"3...
FIA Prod. (28) Carlsson +2'47"8

SS4 Rheola I (32,58 km)
1.Solberg 17'58"6; 2.Loeb +8"5;
3.Mäkinen +17"2; 4.C. McRae +21"3;
5.Panizzi +28"0; 6.Rovanperä +35"1;
7.Gardemeister +41"9; 8.Kresta +44"6...
FIA Prod. (24) Carlsson +2'29"6

SS5 Resolfen I (43,09 km)
1.Solberg 22'40"9; 2.Loeb +3"1;
3.Mäkinen +21"9; 4.C. McRae +25"8;
5.Rovanperä +36"4; 6.Panizzi +43"7;
7.Kresta +58"2; 8.Pykalisto +58"6...
FIA Prod. (20) Carlsson +3'07"8

SS6 Rheola II (32,58 km)
1.Loeb 17'50"9; 2.Solberg +1"6;
3.C. McRae +2"3; 4.Mäkinen +12"5
5.Rovanperä +21"1; 6.Loix +25"0;
7.Panizzi +28"9; 8.Duval +35"4...
FIA Prod. (20) Tirabassi +2'18"8

SS7 Cardiff Super Sp 2 (2,45 km)
1.Solberg 2'06"4; 2.Mäkinen +1"1;
3.C. McRae +1"7; 4.Loeb +1"8;
5.Duval +2"2; 6.Pykalisto +3"0;
7.Rovanperä +3"3; 8.Loix +3"4...
FIA Prod. (28) Baldacci +15"0

SS8 Crychan I (13,05 km)
1.Solberg 7'10"6; 2.Loeb +4"0;
3.C. McRae +5"0; 4.Mäkinen +5"4;
5.Rovanperä +9"8; 6.Duval +10"9;
7.Stohl +13"0; 8.Loix +13"3...
FIA Prod. (16) Carlsson +55"5

SS9 Halfway I (18,53 km)
1.Solberg 10'15"7; 2.Loeb +2"7;
3.Mäkinen +5"0; 4.C. McRae +5"4;
5.Rovanperä +14"8; 6.Loix +15"7;
7.Stohl +17"1; 8.Sola +17"8...
FIA Prod. (17) Carlsson +1'10"3

SS10 Crychan II (13,05 km)
1.Solberg 7'08"0; 2.C. McRae +2"9;
3.Loeb +5"6; 4.Mäkinen +5"7;
5.Loix +8"7; 6.Duval +9"7;
7.Rovanperä +10"3; 8.Stohl +12"2...
FIA Prod. (19) Carlsson +54"6

SS11 Halfway II (18,53 km)
1.Solberg 10'11"0; 2.Loeb +4"4;
3.Mäkinen +5"3; 4.C. McRae +8"5
5.Duval +14"5; 6.Rovanperä +14"7;
7.Loix +15"9; 8.Sola +19"0...
FIA Prod. (17) Meeke +1'07"6

SS12 Margam Forest (17,37 km)
1.Solberg 9'57"7; 2.Loeb +0"1;
3.C. McRae +2"6; 4.Mäkinen +4"5;
5.Rovanperä +12"2; 6.Duval +12"9;
7.Stohl +14"7; 8.Pykalisto +19"0...
FIA Prod. (20) Sola +1'16"0

SS13 Margam Park I (12,64 km)
1.Solberg 7'08"8; 2.Mäkinen +5"8;
3.C. McRae +6"1; 4.Loeb +6"5;
5.Duval +14"5; 6.Rovanperä +16"4;
7.Loix +17"5; 8.Stohl +18"2...
FIA Prod. (17) Meeke +56"2

SS14 Resolfen II (43,09 km)
1.Solberg 22'21"3; 2.Loeb +9"5;
3.C. McRae +16"0; 4.Mäkinen +19"8;
5.Rovanperä +31"2; 6.Loix +36"0;
7.Kresta +48"3; 8.Duval +54"6...
FIA Prod. (17) Carlsson +2'57"3

SS15 Cardiff Super Sp 3 (2,45 km)
1.Solberg 2'05"1; 2.Loeb +0"4;
3.C. McRae +1"3; 4.Mäkinen +1"5;
5.Duval +1"7; 6.Loix +2"6;
7.Rovanperä +3"3; 8.Stohl +3"4...
FIA Prod. (24) Meeke +13"4

SS16 Rhondda I (30,61 km)
1.Loeb 16'25"5; 2.Solberg +5"2;
3.Mäkinen +10"1; 4.C. McRae +12"4;
5.Stohl +24"2; 6.Kresta +30"7;
7.Duval +31"9; 8.Loix +40"3...
FIA Prod. (14) Meeke +2'01"7

SS17 Rhondda II (30,61 km)
1.Loeb 16'21"1; 2.Solberg +3"5;
3.Mäkinen +13"0; 4.C. McRae +14"7;
5.Stohl +38"0; 6.Kresta +41"6;
7.Loix +42"7; 8.Duval +43"7...
FIA Prod. (15) Carlsson +2'03"8

SS18 Margam Park II (12,64 km)
1.Solberg 7'07"4; 2.Loeb +11"1;
3.Duval +15"5; 4.Stohl +19"1;
5.Mäkinen +19"2; 6.Kresta +22"5;
7.Loix +23"0; 8.Pykalisto +27"1...
FIA Prod. (14) Carlsson +1'02"0

Championship Classifications

FIA Drivers (14/14)
1.Solberg 72; 2.Loeb 71; 3.Sainz 63; 4.Burns 58; 5.Märtin 49; 6.Grönholm 46;
7.C. McRae 45; 8.Duval 30; 9.Mäkinen 30; 10.Panizzi 27; 11.Rovanperä 18;
12.Gardemeister 9; 13.Auriol 4; 14.Loix 4; 15.Robert 3; 16.A. McRae 3;
17.Hirvonen 3; 18.Schwarz 3; 19.Tuohino 2; 20.Stohl 2; 21.Ginley 1;
22.Lindholm 1; 23.Bugalski 1; 24.Kresta 1

FIA Constructors (14/14)
1.Citroën 160; 2.Peugeot 145; 3.Subaru 109; 4.Ford 93; 5.Skoda 23; 6.Hyundai 12

FIA Junior WRC (7/7)
1.Tirabassi 38; 2.Canellas 36; 3.Carlsson 23; 4.Aava 20; 5.Baldacci 20;
6.Teuronen 19; 7.Wilks 18; 8.Broccoli 13; 9.Katajamäki 10; 10.Ligato 10;
11.Meeke 8; 12.Iliev 8; 13.Cecchettini 8; 14.Ceccato 8; 15.Feghali 7;
16.Svedlund 5; 17.Sebalj 3; 18.Harrach 1

FIA Production Car WRC (7/7)
1.Rowe 43; 2.Arai 38; 3.Blomqvist 30; 4.Singh 30; 5.Sola 22; 6.McShea 18;
7.Ligato 13; 8.Kulig 11; 9.Trivino 8; 10.Colsoul 7; 11.Al Wahaibi 6; 12.Roman 6;
13.Errani 6; 14.Bourne 5; 15.Manfrinato 5; 16.De Dominicis 4; 17.Ferreyros 4;
18.Holowczyc 4; 19.Aur 2; 20.Sztuka 2; 21.Marrini 1; 22.Richard 1

Performers

	1	2	3	4	5	6
Solberg	13	5	-	-	-	-
Loeb	5	9	1	2	-	1
Mäkinen	-	2	7	7	1	1
C. McRae	-	1	7	6	1	-
Märtin	-	1	2	-	-	-
Grönholm	-	-	1	1	-	-
Duval	-	-	1	-	4	3
Stohl	-	-	-	1	2	-
Rovanperä	-	-	-	-	6	4
Sainz	-	-	-	-	2	-
Loix	-	-	-	-	1	5
Panizzi	-	-	-	-	1	1
Kresta	-	-	-	-	-	3
Pykalisto	-	-	-	-	-	1

Event Leaders

SS1	Solberg
SS2 > SS3	Loeb
SS4 > SS18	Solberg

Previous winners

1974	Mäkinen - Liddon Ford Escort RS 1600
1975	Mäkinen - Liddon Ford Escort RS
1976	Clark - Pegg Ford Escort RS
1977	Waldegaard - Thorszelius Ford Escort RS
1978	Mikkola - Hertz Ford Escort RS
1979	Mikkola - Hertz Ford Escort RS
1980	Toivonen - White Talbot Sunbeam Lotus
1981	Mikkola - Hertz Audi Quattro
1982	Mikkola - Hertz Audi Quattro
1983	Blomqvist - Cederberg Audi Quattro
1984	Vatanen - Harryman Peugeot 205 T16
1985	Toivonen - Wilson Lancia Delta S4
1986	Salonen - Harjanne Peugeot 205 T16
1987	Kankkunen - Piironen Lancia Delta HF
1988	Alen - Kivimaki Lancia Delta Integrale

1989	Airikkala - McNamee Mitsubishi Galant VR4
1990	Sainz - Moya Toyota Celica GT-Four
1991	Kankkunen - Piironen Lancia Delta Integrale
1992	Sainz - Moya Toyota Celica Turbo 4WD
1993	Kankkunen - Piironen Toyota Celica Turbo 4WD
1994	McRae - Ringer Subaru Impreza
1995	McRae - Ringer Subaru Impreza
1996	Schwarz - Giraudet Toyota Celica GT-Four
1997	McRae - Grist Subaru Impreza WRC
1998	Burns - Reid Mitsubishi Carisma GT
1999	Burns - Reid Subaru Impreza WRC
2000	Burns - Reid Subaru Impreza WRC 2000
2001	Gronhölm - Rautiainen Peugeot 206 WRC
2002	Solberg - Mills Subaru Impreza WRC 2002

Daniel Carlsson

2003 FIA World Rally Championship / Drivers

24 DRIVERS / 60	Nationalities	Monte Carlo	Sweden	Turkey	New Zealand	Argentina	Greece	Cyprus	Germany	Finland	Australia	Italy	France	Spain	Great Britain	POINTS
1. Petter Solberg	(FIN)	-	3	-	6	4	6	10	1	8	10	-	10	4	10	72
2. Sébastien Loeb	(F)	10	2	-	5	-	-	6	10	4	8	10	0	8	8	71
3. Carlos Sainz	(E)	6	0	10	0	8	8	4	3	5	4	5	8	2	-	63
4. Richard Burns	(GB)	4	6	8	8	6	5	-	6	6	6	2	1	0	-	58
5. Markko Märtin	(EE)	5	5	3	-	-	10	-	4	10	-	6	-	6	-	49
6. Marcus Grönholm	(FIN)	0	10	0	10	10	-	-	8	-	-	-	5	3	-	46
7. Colin McRae	(GB)	8	4	5	-	-	1	5	5	-	5	3	4	0	5	45
8. Tommi Mäkinen	(FIN)	-	8	1	2	-	4	-	-	3	3	0	2	1	6	30
9. François Duval	(B)	2	-	6	0	1	-	-	2	-	0	4	6	5	4	30
10. Gilles Panizzi	(F)	-	4			2		-	0			8	3	10	-	27
11. Harri Rovanperä	(FIN)					5	3	8		-	2				-	18
12. Toni Gardemeister	(FIN)	-	1	2	4	2	-	-	-	-	0		0	0	-	9
13. Didier Auriol	(F)	0	0	-	1	3	0	-	-	-	0	0	-	-	0	4
14. Freddy Loix	(B)	-	0	0	-	-	-	-	0	0	1				3	4
15. Cédric Robert	(F)	3						0			0	0	0			3
16. Mikko Hirvonen	(FIN)	-	0	-	0	0	-	3	0	-	0		0	0	-	3
17. Alister Mcrae	(GB)	°	°	°	3											3
18. Armin Schwarz	(D)	1	0	-	-	-	-	2	0	0	0					3
19. Manfred Stohl	(A)	°			-		0		0				-		2	2
20. Janne Tuohino	(FIN)	°	°	°	°	°	°	°	°	2						2
21. Philippe Bugalski	(F)				°					°		1	0	0		1
22. Roman Kresta	(CZ)	0	0			-		-			0		0	1		1
23. Alistair Ginley	(GB)		0	°		0	1	-	0			-	0	-		1
24. Sebastian Lindholm	(FIN)			°				°	1							1

Toshihiro Arai (J), Juuso Pykalisto (FIN), Jari-Matti Latvala (FIN), Martin Rowe (GB), Gabriel Raies (RA), Anthony Warmbold (D), Stig Blomqvist (S), Ari Vatanen (FIN), Daniel Sola Vila (E), Tobias Johansson (S), Kristian Sohlberg (FIN), Marcus Ligato (RA), Olivier Burri (CH), Karamjit Singh (MAL), Balazs Benik (H), Geof Argyle (NZ), Charalambos Timotheou (CY), Nicolas Bernadi (F), Simon Jean-Joseph (F), Bob Colsoul (B), Ioannis Papadimitriou (GR), Giovanni Manfrinato (I), Daniel Carlsson (S), Bruce Herbert (NZ), Xavier Pons (E), Eamonn Boland (IRL), Kosti Katajamäki (FIN), Kristian Kolberg (N), Cody Crocker (AUS), Federico Villagra (RA), Yiotis Hartoupalos (CY), Matthias Kahle (D), Juha Salo (FIN), Piero Liatti (I), Mark Higgins (GB), Mirco Baldacci (RSM)

2003 FIA World Rally Championship / Constructors

CONSTRUCTORS	Nationalities	Monte Carlo	Sweden	Turkey	New Zealand	Argentina	Greece	Cyprus	Germany	Finland	Australia	Italy	France	Spain	Great Britain	POINTS
1. Citroën	(F)	18	6	15	5	8	10	11	15	9	13	15	12	10	13	160
2. Peugeot	(F)	6	16	9	18	16	8	8	14	6	9	11	8	13	3	145
3. Subaru	(ROK)	0	11	2	9	5	10	10	2	11	14	2	12	5	16	109
4. Ford	(GB)	10	5	10	1	3	10	4	7	10	1	10	7	11	4	93
5. Skoda	(CZ)	2	1	3	6	7	1	0	0	0	0	1	0	0	2	23
6. Hyundai	(ROK)	3	0	0	0	0	0	3	1	3	2					12

REGULATIONS: DRIVERS' CHAMPIONSHIP: All result count. 1st - 10 points, 2nd - 8 points, 3rd - 6 points, 4th - 5 points, 5th - 4 points, 6th - 3 points, 7th - 2 points, 8th - 1 point.
CONSTRUCTORS' CHAMPIONSHIP: To be eligible, the constructors who have registered with FIA, must take part in all the events with a minimum of two cars. The first two cars score the points according to their finishing position. All results are taken into consideration. Points scale is the same as for the drivers.

World Championship for Constructors

1973 Alpine-Renault	1980 Fiat	1988 Lancia	1996 Subaru
1974 Lancia	1981 Talbot	1989 Lancia	1997 Subaru
1975 Lancia	1982 Audi	1990 Lancia	1998 Mitsubishi
1976 Lancia	1983 Lancia	1991 Lancia	1999 Toyota
1977 Fiat	1984 Audi	1992 Lancia	2000 Peugeot
1978 Fiat	1985 Peugeot	1993 Toyota	2001 Peugeot
1979 Ford	1986 Peugeot	1994 Toyota	2002 Peugeot
	1987 Lancia	1995 Subaru	2003 Citroën

World Championship for Drivers

1977 Sandro Munari (I)	1991 Juha Kankkunen (SF)
1978 Markku Alen (SF)	1992 Carlos Sainz (E)
1979 Bjorn Waldegaard (S)	1993 Juha Kankkunen (SF)
1980 Walter Rohrl (D)	1994 Didier Auriol (F)
1981 Ari Vatanen (SF)	1995 Colin McRae (GB)
1982 Walter Rohrl (D)	1996 Tommi Makinen (SF)
1983 Hannu Mikkola (SF)	1997 Tommi Makinen (SF)
1984 Stig Blomqvist (S)	1998 Tommi Makinen (SF)
1985 Timo Salonen (SF)	1999 Tommi Makinen (SF)
1986 Juha Kankkunen (SF)	2000 Marcus Grönholm (SF)
1987 Juha Kankkunen (SF)	2001 Richard Burns (GB)
1988 Miki Biasion (I)	2002 Marcus Grönholm (SF)
1989 Miki Biasion (I)	2003 Petter Solberg (N)
1990 Carlos Sainz (E)	

1977-1978: FIA Cup for drivers

2003 FIA Production Car World Rally Championship (for drivers)

	DRIVERS	Nationalities	Sweden	New Zealand	Argentina	Cyprus	Germany	Australia	France	POINTS
1.	Martin Rowe	(GB)	6	5		8	8	10	6	43
2.	Toshihiro Arai	(J)	-	10	10	10		-	8	38
3.	Stig Blomqvist	(S)	10	1		6	4	5	4	30
4.	Karamjit Singh	(MAL)	8	3	6	-	5	8		30
5.	Daniel Sola	(E)	-	0	8	-	10	4		22
6.	Niall Mcshea	(GB)	-	2		-	-	6	10	18
7.	Marcos Ligato	(RA)	-	8	-	5	-	-		13
8.	Janusz Kulig	(PL)	-	-	-	-	6		5	11
9.	Ricardo Trivino	(MEX)	-	0	3	-	3		2	8
10.	Bob Colsoul	(B)	0	-	-	4	-		3	7
11.	Hamed Al Wahaibi	(OM)	-	6						6
12.	Joakim Roman	(S)	3	0		-	-	3	0	6
13.	Riccardo Errani	(I)			2	3	0		1	6
14.	Giovanni Manfrinato	(I)	-	0	5	-	-			5
15.	Possum Bourne	(NZ)	5	-						5
16.	Alfredo De Dominicis	(I)	0	0	4	-			-	4
17.	Krysztof Holowczyc	(PL)	4	-		-	-			4
18.	Ramon Ferreyros	(PE)	-	4	-	-	-	-	-	4
19.	Lukasz Sztuka	(PL)	2	-	-					2
20.	Titi Aur	(R)	-	-	-	-	2	-		2
21.	Stefano Marrini	(I)	-	-	-	-	1	-	0	1
22.	Patrick Richard	(CDN)	1	-	-	-	-	-	-	1
23.	Luca Baldini	(I)	0	-	-					0
24.	Georgi Geradzhiev	(BG)	0	0	-	-	-			0
25.	Stanislav Chovanec	(CZ)	-	-	-					0

Production Car Championship (Gr. N)

1987 Alex Fiorio (I)
1995 Rui Madeira (PT)
1988 Pascal Gaban (B)
1996 Gustavo Trelles (ROU)
1989 Alain Oreille (F)
1997 Gustavo Trelles (ROU)
1990 Alain Oreille (F)
1998 Gustavo Trelles (ROU)
1991 Grégoire de Mevius (B)
1999 Gustavo Trelles (ROU)
1992 Grégoire de Mevius (B)
2000 Manfred Stohl (D)
1993 Alex Fassina (I)
2001 Gabriel Pozzo (RA)
1994 Jesus Puras (E)
2002 Karamjit Singh (MAL)
2003 Martin Rowe (GB)

2003 FIA Junior World Rally Championship (for drivers)

	DRIVERS	Nationalities	Monte Carlo	Turkey	Greece	Finland	Italy	Spain	Great Britain	POINTS
1.	Brice Tirabassi	(F)	10	-	10	8		10	-	38
2.	Savador Canellas	(E)	-	8	5	4	8	6	5	36
3.	Daniel Carlsson	(S)	-		8	10	-	5	10	33
4.	Mirco Baldacci	(RSM)	2	-			10	-	8	20
5.	Urmo Aava	(EE)	5	-	6	5	-	4	-	20
6.	Ville-Pertti Teuronen	(FIN)	-	5			5	3	6	19
7.	Guy Wilks	(GB)	-	6	3	6	3	0	-	18
8.	Alessandro Broccoli	(RSM)	6	-		3	-	-	4	13
9.	Kosti Katajamäki	(FIN)		10			-	-	-	10
10.	Marcos Ligato	(RA)	8	-		2	-			10
11.	Kris Meeke	(GB)	0	-		-	8			8
12.	Dimitar Iliev	(BG)	-	2		6	-			8
13.	Luca Cecchettini	(I)	0	4		4	0	-		8
14.	Massimo Ceccato	(I)	4	-		-	1	3		8
15.	Abdorl Feghali	(RL)	0	3		2	2	-		7
16.	Oscar Svedlund	(S)			4	1	-	-		5
17.	Juraj Sebalj	(CR)	3							3
18.	Beppo Harrach	(A)	1	-						1
19.	Krum Donchev	(BG)	0	-		-	0			0

World Junior Championship

2001 Sébastien Loeb (F)
2002 Daniel Sola (E)
2003 Brice Tirabassi (F)

Sébastien Ceccone (F), Dariusz Chubobinski (PL), David Dopplereiter (A), Kristian Sohlberg (FIN), Martin Stenshorne (N), Filippo Suessli (CH), Jader Vagnini (RSM), Pavel Valousek (CZ), Vladan Vasiljevic (D)   0

DRIVERS WHO HAVE WON WORLD CHAMPIONSHIP RALLIES FROM 1973 TO 2003

DRIVERS	NATIONALITIES	Nbr. of WINS	RALLIES
Andrea Aghini	(I)	1	1992 I
Pentti Airikkala	(FIN)	1	1989 GB
Markku Alen	(FIN)	20	1975 PT • 1976 FIN • 1977 PT • 1978 PT, FIN, I • 1979 FIN • 1980 FIN • 1981 PT • 1983 F, I • 1984 F • 1986 I, USA • 1987 PT, GR, FIN • 1988 S, FIN, GB
Alain Ambrosino	(F)	1	1988 CI
Ove Andersson	(S)	1	1975 EAK
Jean-Claude Andruet	(F)	3	1973 MC • 1974 F • 1977 I
Didier Auriol	(F)	20	1988 F • 1989 F • 1990 MC, F, I • 1991 I • 1992 MC, F, GR, RA, FIN, AUS • 1993 MC • 1994 F, RA, I • 1995 F • 1998 E • 1999 C • 2001 E
Fulvio Bacchelli	(I)	1	1977 NZ
Bernard Beguin	(F)	1	1987 F
Miki Biasion	(I)	17	1986 RA • 1987 MC, RA, I • 1988 PT, EAK, GR, USA, I • 1989 MC, PT, EAK, GR, I • 1990 PT, RA • 1993 GR
Stig Blomqvist	(S)	11	1973 S • 1977 S • 1979 S • 1982 S, I • 1983 GB • 1984 S, GR, NZ, RA, CI
Walter Boyce	(CDN)	1	1973 USA
Philippe Bugalski	(F)	2	1999 E, F
Richard Burns	(GB)	9	1998 EAK • 1999 GR, AUS, GB • 2000 EAK, PT, RA, GB • 2001 NZ
Ingvar Carlsson	(S)	2	1989 S, NZ
Roger Clark	(GB)	1	1976 GB
Gianfranco Cunico	(I)	1	1993 I
Bernard Darniche	(F)	7	1973 MA • 1975 F • 1977 F • 1978 F • 1979 MC, F • 1981 F
François Delecour	(F)	4	1993 PT, F, E • 1994 MC
Ian Duncan	(EAK)	1	1994 EAK
Per Eklund	(S)	1	1976 S
Mikael Ericsson	(S)	2	1989 RA, FIN
Kenneth Eriksson	(S)	6	1987 CI • 1991 S • 1995 S, AUS • 1997 S, NZ
Tony Fassina	(I)	1	1979 I
Guy Frequelin	(F)	1	1981 RA
Marcus Grönholm	(FIN)	15	2000 S, NZ, F, AUS • 2001 FIN, AUS, GB • 2002 S, CY, FIN, NZ, AUS • 2003 S, NZ, RA
Sepp Haider	(A)	1	1988 NZ
Kyosti Hamalainen	(FIN)	1	1977 FIN
Mats Jonsson	(S)	2	1992 S • 1993 S
Harry Kallstom	(S)	1	1976 GR
Juha Kankkunen	(FIN)	23	1985 EAK, CI • 1986 S, GR, NZ • 1987 USA, GB • 1989 AUS • 1990 AUS • 1991 EAK, GR, FIN, AUS, GB • 1992 PT • 1993 EAK, RA, FIN, AUS, GB • 1994 PT • 1999 RA, FIN
Anders Kullang	(S)	1	1980 S
Piero Liatti	(I)	1	1997 MC
Sébastien Loeb	(F)	4	2002 D • 2003 MC, D, I
Colin McRae	(GB)	25	1993 NZ • 1994 NZ, GB • 1995 NZ, GB • 1996 GR, I, E • 1997 EAK, F, I, AUS, GB • 1998 PT, F, GR • 1999 EAK, PT • 2000 E, GR • 2001 ARG, CY, GR • 2002 GR, EAK
Timo Makinen	(FIN)	4	1973 FIN, GB • 1974 GB • 1975 GB
Tommi Mäkinen	(FIN)	24	1994 FIN • 1996 S, EAK, RA, FIN, AUS • 1997 PT, E, RA, FIN • 1998 S, RA, NZ, FIN, I, AUS • 1999 Mc, S, NZ, I • 2000 MC • 2001 MC, POR, EAK • 2002 MC
Markko Märtin	(EE)	2	2003 GR, FIN
Shekhar Mehta	(EAK)	5	1973 EAK • 1979 EAK • 1980 EAK • 1981 EAK • 1982 EAK
Hannu Mikkola	(FIN)	18	1974 FIN • 1975 MA, FIN • 1978 GB • 1979 PT, NZ, GB, CI • 1981 S, GB • 1982 FIN, GB • 1983 S, PT, RA, FIN 1984 PT • 1987 EAK
Joaquim Moutinho	(PT)	1	1986 PT
Michèle Mouton	(F)	4	1981 I • 1982 PT, GR, BR
Sandro Munari	(I)	7	1974 I, CDN • 1975 MC • 1976 MC, PT, F • 1977 MC
Jean-Pierre Nicolas	(F)	5	1973 F • 1976 MA • 1978 MC, EAK, CI
Alain Oreille	(F)	1	1989 CI
Jesus Puras	(E)	1	2001 FR
Gilles Panizzi	(F)	6	2000 F, I • 2001 IT • 2002 F, E, I • 2003 E
Rafaelle Pinto	(PT)	1	1974 PT
Jean Ragnotti	(F)	3	1981 MC • 1982 F • 1985 F
Jorge Recalde	(RA)	1	1988 RA
Walter Röhrl	(D)	14	1975 GR • 1978 GR, CDN • 1980 MC, PT, RA, I • 1982 MC, CI • 1983 MC, GR, NZ 1984 MC • 1985 I
Harri Rovanperä	(FIN)	1	2001 S
Bruno Saby	(F)	2	1986 F • 1988 MC
Carlos Sainz	(E)	25	1990 GR, NZ, FIN, GB • 1991 MC, PT, F, NZ, RA • 1992 EAK, NZ, E, GB • 1994 GR 1995 MC, PT, E • 1996 RI • 1997 GR, RI • 1998 MC, NZ 2000 CY • 2002 RA • 2003 TR
Timo Salonen	(FIN)	11	1977 CDN • 1980 NZ • 1981 CI • 1985 PT, GR, NZ, RA, FIN • 1986 FIN, GB • 1987 S
Armin Schwarz	(D)	1	1991 E
Kenjiro Shinozuka	(J)	2	1991 CI • 1992 CI
Joginder Singh	(EAK)	2	1974 EAK • 1976 EAK
Petter Solberg	(N)	5	2002 GB • 2003 CY, AUS, F, GB
Patrick Tauziac	(F)	1	1990 CI
Jean-Luc Thèrier	(F)	5	1973 PT, GR, I • 1974 USA • 1980 F
Henri Toivonen	(FIN)	3	1980 GB • 1985 GB • 1986 MC
Ari Vatanen	(FIN)	10	1980 GR • 1981 GR, BR, FIN • 1983 EAK • 1984 FIN, I, GB • 1985 MC, S
Bjorn Waldegaard	(S)	16	1975 S, I • 1976 I • 1977 EAK, GR, GB • 1978 S • 1979 GR, CDN • 1980 CI • 1982 NZ • 1983 CI • 1984 EAK • 1986 EAK, CI • 1990 EAK
Achim Warmbold	(D)	2	1973 PL, A
Franz Wittmann	(A)	1	1987 NZ

A: Austria, AUS: Australia, B: Belgium, BG: Bulgaria, BR: Brazil, C: China, CDN: Canada, CI: Ivory Coast, CY: Cyprus, CZ: Czech Republic, D: Germany, E: Spain, EAK: Kenya, EST: Estonia, F: France, FIN: Finland, GB: Great Britain, GR: Greece, I: Italy, J: Japaon, LT: Lithuania, MA: Morocco, MAL: Malaysia, MC: Monaco, N: Norway, NZ: New Zealand, PE: Peru, PL: Poland, PT: Portugal, PY: Paraguay, RA: Argentina, RI: Indonesia, RL: Leganon, ROK: Republic of Korea, ROU: Uruguay, RSM: San Marino, S: Sweden, TR: Turkey, USA : United States of America

SHARE THE TRIUMPH

www.michelin.com